Porsches For The Road   Henry Rasmussen

PORSCHES FO

Published by Motorbooks International
Publishers and Wholesalers Incorporated,
Osceola, Wisconsin, U.S.A.
Copyright 1981 by Henry Rasmussen.
Library of Congress number 81-11314
ISBN 0-87938-152-3.
Printed in Hong Kong by South China
Printing Company.

Porsche and racing are synonymous. Professor Ferdinand Porsche learned early that racing victories meant free publicity. The House of Porsche never forgot that. By 1953, the factory realized that the stock 356 and the 1.5-liter push-rod engine would not satisfy future racing plans. Enter the 550 Spyder. Karosserie Wendler of Reutlingen built the aluminum body to Porsche's specifications. The design originated with the Glöckler specials, but the final styling was by Erwin Komenda. Dr. Ernst Fuhrmann designed the four-cam engine single-handedly; 1498 cc, 110 DIN hp (125 SAE) at 7500 rpm, with a Hirth roller bearing crank. It was willing and able: 0-60 under ten seconds. But that didn't win races; balance was the key word, and power: top speed 140 mph with flexibility. And handling: one road tester said the center of gravity was below the ground. And brakes: big, finned drums, with stock sixteen-inch 356 wheels and slightly wider tires aft. The engine was mounted ahead of the rear axle with the four-speed synchromesh transmission behind it. Weight was just 1,250 pounds, wheelbase 82.7 inches, and price $6,800. The ladder frame was changed to a tubular one in late 1955 and the model name was changed to 550A. There were changes made right to the end of the Spyder series in 1962. About two hundred examples were made. While Porsche built a strong, reliable touring car in the 356, it was the Spyder that gave it the reputation of a winner. And Porsche sold what it raced. But naturally, the factory was always a little ahead of the purchaser in development.

Affectionately known as the bathtub, the Speedster captured the spirit of Porsche in the United States. It was the idea of Max Hoffman, United States distributor for Porsche, to have a stark price leader. When introduced, the tag was $2,995 in New York City, with some standard equipment at extra cost. This was Hoffman's idea; for Porsche, it was in a sense a step backward. The cabriolet had a padded top and roll-up windows; the Speedster had just a simple canvas top and side curtains. Vision was terrible with the top up. But, with the four-cylinder, air-cooled, push-rod engine, the Speedster was reliable and fast. Fast is relative, but point-to-point distances were covered amazingly quickly. Racing proved this. With the Super 1600 cc engine (actually 1588 cc), power was 75 DIN hp (88 SAE) at 5000 rpm; 0-60 in 10.5 seconds and a top speed just over 100 mph. The car was solid, unlike other sports cars, because of the platform frame with unit body. If a rattle developed, it was something the owner put in or on the car. Each wheel was independently suspended. Wheelbase was 82.7 inches, weight about 1,850 pounds and in 1958 there was also the normal engine, 60 DIN hp (70 SAE) at 4500 rpm and the four-cam engine with plain bearings known as the Carrera. The four-speed, synchromesh transmission was a delight. Braking was through big drums, with a swept area greater than most luxury sedans. The Speedster is raced in vintage racing as well as current SCCA racing. It can win either variety. With ancestors like the Auto Union Grand Prix car and the Volkswagen, how can it miss?

550 Spyder

356A Speedster

Porsche usually made its engines to fit in a racing classification. The original 1086 cc engine fit in the 1100 cc class; the 1582 engine of the later 356s fit into the 1600 cc class. The four-cam engine won races in the 1100 cc, 1500 cc and in the largest version, the 2000 cc class. This four-cam engine was de-tuned and placed in the 356 series. The 1966 cc version engine with plain bearings was put in the B-series and labeled the 356B/2000GS, but was called and labeled the Carrera 2. Homologation called for 100 units, but 320 B-series and 126 C-series cars were actually built. Power was 110 DIN hp (130 SAE) at 6200 rpm. A 0-60 time of 8.7 seconds and a top speed of 125 mph was easily possible. For the added power, disc brakes were fitted all around. Price in the United States was $7,595. Bodies were by Reutter, made with the usual precision. The engine was available in both the coupe and cabriolet. Weight of the coupe was 2,200 pounds. An identifying feature was the skirt under the rear bumper with the twin exhaust pipes protruding. The front grilles, next to the parking lights, were generally omitted. The usual rear engine location with four-speed transmission just in front of the engine was continued. Wheelbase remained 82.7 inches. With the extra power, the Porsche balance remained with the disc brakes. Handling was still tops. The larger four-cam engine now provided more low end torque without any loss of power to maximum revs. It became an ideal Gran Turismo auto for point-to-point driving or racing.

After fifteen years of production in Stuttgart/Zuffenhausen, the 1965 356C was about as different from the 1950 356 as a facelift on a one-year-old Detroit model. The engine was enlarged from 1086 cc to 1582 cc, disc brakes replaced the drums, a fully synchromesh transmission replaced the crash box and the headlights and bumpers were a little higher. However, the car looked similar, had the same platform frame with unit body, retained the 82.7-inch wheelbase, and kept the rear engine with the four-speed transmission in the front of the engine. Only two body styles were available — the coupe and the cabriolet — and just two engines — the 70 DIN hp (88 SAE) at 5000 rpm or the 95 DIN hp (107 SAE) at 5500 rpm. Actually, the 126 Carrera 2 models should be included here, but with 16,668 356Cs produced, their number was almost insignificant. The 95 DIN hp was designated the 356SC and performance was 0-60 in eleven seconds and a top speed of 115 mph. Karosserie Reutter was now absorbed by Porsche. Since 1960 Reutter couldn't keep up with the demand; therefore Karmann complemented production. The cars were still made by hand, more so than any other production auto. The price of the cabriolet was $4,200 in the United States. In the finest European tradition, it still had a padded top with bows covered by a headliner and was very snug. It was not a fussy car, still able to thread a needle in traffic; fast, yet economical. It didn't need 300 hp to attain 100 mph nor did it need power steering or even power brakes.

356 B Carrera 2

356 SC Cabriolet

A fiberglass Porsche for street and racing! With a steel-box frame which was strengthened by bonding to the body, many say the 904 was the most beautiful Porsche made. Styling was by Ferdinand (Butzi) Porsche III and the body was made by Ernst Heinkel Flugzeugbau. Fiberglass was chosen for lower weight and the small production run planned. While 100 units were needed for homologation, 110 cars were actually made. The body came in three sections: the hood, the tail and the cockpit. The engine compartment was planned for the six-cylinder racing engine. It wasn't ready in time, so the Fuhrmann four-cylinder, four-cam engine went in. Two stages were available — for the street, 155 hp at 6400 rpm; for racing, 180 hp at 7200 rpm. Displacement was the same as the Carrera 2 at 1966 cc. Engine placement was right behind the seat, midship. The five-speed transmission was aft, a repeat of all racing cars from Porsche. The racing engine would propel the 904 from 0-60 in 5.6 seconds and a top speed of 160 mph. Price at the factory was $7,425. The 904 was only 41.9 inches high and weighed 1,430 pounds. Braking was by four-wheel discs. The light alloy, five-inch-wide rims were mounted with Dunlop SP 165x15 radials. Wheelbase was 90.6 inches. Most 904s were sold in racing form. The factory raced some 904s with six-cylinder engines, and some with eights. Some 904s were seen in open versions, but the long, clean silver coupe with the bobbed tail was the usual version. In 1964, the Carrera GTS took first and second places at the Targa Florio. Many other victories followed.

Actually, Porsche Design 912 was the engine for the fabulous 917 race car. The road car called 912 just happened to be the number after 911. Porsche Design 901 was actually the new six-cylinder engine. But Peugeot held the rights to use combinations where the middle number was a zero, causing Porsche to change to 911. The 912 was the 911 with the old four-cylinder push-rod 1588 cc engine producing 90 DIN hp (102 SAE). Obviously, it was not as fast as the 911 — as a matter of fact it was slow: 0-60 in 11.5 seconds and a top speed of 115 mph. Disc brakes were used all around and it had a wheelbase of 89.3 inches on the 1969 model. The car was available as a coupe or Targa model. The 912 occupied the lowest step on the price ladder. In 1965, the United States price started at $4,745 and by 1969 it had gone up to $5,200 — base price for the coupe. About 30,000 912s were made. Styling was by Butzi Porsche. It retained the basic look of the 356 but had more room for passengers and luggage. Although Reutter had since been absorbed by Porsche, and the factory built the 911 bodies, the 912 was usually built by Karosserie Karmann. The 911 was sold for a year before the first 912 became available. The first few 912s had a painted dashboard with only three instruments, just like the 356C. With the built-in flexibility of a Porsche, the 912 could still gobble up the miles rapidly. On club tours, the 911 would only be able to pull away if there was a long straightaway. The 912 kept a lot of people driving Porsches who couldn't have afforded a 911. That was one of its purposes.

904 Carrera GTS

912

"You can't win them all," stated a Porsche ad for the 914/6. It listed eleven wins out of twelve starts in C Production SCCA racing. The 914 was the low-priced Porsche, replacing the 912. The 914/6 was the expensive 914. The car was made in arrangement with Volkswagen. Karosserie Karmann made the 96.5-inch wheelbase body, based on a design by Gugelot Design of Neu-Ulm. Most bodies received the VW Type IV engine; however, a small number of bodies went to Stuttgart/Zuffenhausen to receive 911 engines and running gear. The 1969 911T 1991 cc engine was placed midship. With two triple-throat Weber carburetors, the engine produced 110 DIN hp (125 SAE) at 5800 rpm. The 914/6 had four-wheel disc brakes, a five-speed synchromesh transmission and weighed 2,250 pounds. Externally, small script on the rear panel and five-lug wheels were the clues to the 914/6. The fourteen-inch Fuchs alloy wheels were usually fitted. As delivered, it would do 0-60 in 8.2 seconds and top out at 125 mph. The price in the United States was $6,000, just a few dollars shy of the 2.2-liter 911T. Because of that, sales were disappointing. The 914/6GT with larger engine and mean-looking fender flares didn't help sales. Even a planned series of 916s — a fixed-head coupe, with new nose and rear panels — got no further than eleven cars. Demand dwindled and production faded in 1971 just after 3,362 914/6s had been made. Sales continued until 1972. A funny thing happened: With no more new 914/6s available, they became more popular. The mid-engined, four-cylinder 914 lasted until 1976.

The cost of racing the potent 917 was tremendous; however, the publicity of winning races justified that cost. Still, Ernst Fuhrmann, the new president of Porsche, looked for a less expensive route. He saw that with a little magic, the ten-year-old 911 could become a winner. The result was the Carrera RS — a production-based car. Take one six-cylinder 911 and increase the engine size to 2687 cc and the power to 210 DIN hp (230 SAE), add the 911E/S front spoiler and a ducktail rear spoiler, reduce the weight and build five hundred examples to qualify for homologation. It was that simple; actually, sales topped 1,800 units, even without the United States market, which was eliminated due to emission regulations. The sales impetus allowed its inclusion in Group 4 racing as well as the planned Group 3 racing. In February 1973, an RSR was the overall Daytona winner. The Carrera RS used the platform frame and unit body resting on an 89.3-inch wheelbase, and it weighed 2,000 pounds. Suspension, in Porsche tradition, was all-independent. The rear spoiler actually worked — it reduced rear lift from 320 pounds at 150 mph to just 93 pounds, with a plus of increasing airflow in the engine compartment. Performance — how about 0-60 in 5.5 seconds and top speed of 150 mph? Wheel width was six inches with four-wheel disc brakes. Price, about $12,500. Of note are the graphics. Decals weigh nothing; red or blue ones on a white car spelled out Carrera, in reverse lettering. Matching color Fuchs alloy wheels completed the effect.

914-6

911 Carrera RS

Would you consider rare, a model that was produced in only 174 units? In 1975, that's the total number of 911 Carrera Targas. Only thirty-six were painted gold on black. The 911 Carrera was a mean-looking machine, with the larger wheels, fender flares and that big "whale-tail." In the United States, the Carrera was the top of the line. The plain 911 was dropped, and lowest-priced 911 became the 911S. For once, the two models had the same engine (in the United States). Both were rated at 157 SAE hp (152 in California) at 5800 rpm. Performance was 0-60 in 8.4 seconds and a top speed of 137 mph, just 134 for the 911S due to the whale-tail. Gone was the usual Porsche separation of models by horsepower. The Carrera in the United States was a trim option: standard was five-speed transmission, front and rear spoiler, flared fenders, seven-inch front and eight-inch rear, painted alloys, black trim including the roll bar, leather seats and velour carpeting. It still kept the twelve-year-old body, with an 89.4-inch wheelbase, unit construction, and weighing about 2,370 pounds. The Targa, named after numerous victories in the Sicilian Targa Florio, was introduced in 1967. At that time, it had a roll bar, removable top and plastic rear window. There were four possibilities: closed, top off, rear window down, and top off and rear window down. Later, the plastic rear window was replaced by a glass window. Sales of the 1975 Porsche 911 didn't slacken, even with the gas crunch, higher prices and the rumor of a new liquid-cooled, front-engined Porsche.

It seems like turbocharging was invented by Porsche. Actually, the principle goes back to 1905, when a patent was given to Swiss engineer Alfred Buchi; ten years later he got another patent more in keeping with the current application. In World War II, aircraft engines used the turbo; then came the Indianapolis-type race cars in the fifties. In 1962, Oldsmobile introduced a turbo V-8. Porsche's first turbo was the 917-10 Can Am car in 1972. Turbocharging made a championship car, the 917, a terror. After 1973, Porsche developed the turbo for the 911 engine. Turbocharging is simply routing the exhaust gases back into the engine. The wastegate bypasses the gases around the turbine, thus limiting boost. The good, old 911 received a shot in the tail with the turbo. By 1979, the last year the 930 was sold by Porsche in the United States, the 3299 cc six-cylinder engine was putting out 261 SAE hp at 5500 rpm. Performance was 0-60 in about six seconds and a top speed of 155 mph. The car could be like a little lamb, very docile and even a little old lady would have no trouble driving it. The tiger in it required only a heavy foot. Where the regular 911S would run out of horsepower, the Turbo merely slammed you back in the seat. Only four speeds were necessary. Production never exceeded six hundred units a year. The last fifty 930 Turbos brought into the United States had special plaques with Ferry Porsche's signature. They were called "signature edition." Porsche still makes the 930, but not for United States consumption. The 930 Turbo is the ultimate Porsche, still maintaining balance, precision and technology.

911 Carrera Targa

930 Turbo

The 928 started life on a clean sheet of paper. It was targeted for the mature buyer who was weaned on sports cars. The front-mounted, liquid-cooled engine displaces 4473 cc, has a single overhead cam, is a V-8 and produces 219 SAE hp at 5250 rpm. Performance is very pleasing: 0-60 in seven seconds and a top speed of 138 mph. The rear transaxle can be ordered with either five-speed manual or fully automatic transmission. The rear axle is special; it is called the Weissach axle and aids the driver by actually turning into the corner. Weight distribution is 50/50. Handling is superior to the 911. Wheelbase is 98.3 inches and the weight is 3,410 pounds. Tony Lapine, an American who heads the styling studio at Porsche, and his staff styled the body. It is built at the factory. In Europe, the 928 was named "Car of the Year" when introduced. In the United States, the car was originally priced at $26,000. Porsche has chosen to keep secret how good the 928 really is. A drive in the car is sheer delight. The front and rear sections have an aluminum substructure covered by polyurethane, painted to match the body. The biggest, heaviest, most luxurious Porsche retains the intricate balance that is Porsche's. It may be the best Porsche yet. Keeping with tradition, a 928S has been introduced in Europe, featuring increased power and improved handling. There's even a vestigial spoiler below the rear window. Porsche owners have always asked for more power and the factory has always responded. Can homologation and racing of the 928 be far away? And how about a turbo version?

The 924, presented in late 1976, was a totally new Porsche. It broke the tradition of rear-engined, air-cooled cars with a bang. Porsche stated that the price was "not inexpensive." It was, nevertheless, the least expensive Porsche. In a sense, it is like the 356 made in Gmünd, Austria; it uses production parts from other automobiles, the VW and the Audi. The transaxle is similar to one Professor Porsche designed for Mercedes-Benz. Since Butzi Porsche had left the factory, the styling of the car was in the hands of Tony Lapine. The 924 uses a front-mounted, four-cylinder, single overhead cam engine, also used by Audi. In turbo form, it displaces 1984 cc, puts out 154 SAE hp at 5500 rpm and tops out at 130 mph, with a 0-60 time of 9.2 seconds. Wheelbase is 94.5 inches and weight is 2,850 pounds. Judged by numbers made, the 924 is the most successful Porsche; production has already topped 100,000 units. Cost of the Turbo is $21,500, base price, United States. Besides the Turbo series, there have been several special versions offered, each with special colors and options: the Championship Edition in white with red and blue striping, celebrating the double World Championship in 1976; the Limited Edition in gray; the Sebring Edition in red, copying the Sebring pace car; the Weissach Edition in platinum; and the Carrera GT series. In the now-familiar required number of production units for homologation, four hundred Carrera GTs were made, but are not for sale in the United States. In the future, maybe the polyurethane fenders from the Carrera GT will be used on a new production version.

928

924 Turbo

Essence of a Sports Car

Most enthusiasts agree on what makes a car a sports car. Sure, there are extreme opinions. Yes, there are some who would only consider the most exotic. And there are those who would accept anything that moves fast and lacks a muffler.

Yes, there are extremes. But the majority agree that a sports car should be relatively small, have an intimate cockpit, should be fast, fun to drive, handle well, should be low and beautiful in a sensuous way — and have a sound to match.

One winter night, I think it was in 1953 — I was still a teenager in Sweden then — a major rally passed not far from where I lived. I was, of course, among the spectators, watching the cars negotiate a ninety-degree curve at the top of a hill. The road was icy and they needed speed to get to the top, but not too much, or they would overshoot the turn and end up in a deep ravine. I watched the cars all night as they passed in a steady stream, exploding the stillness of the night, sliding sideways through the curve with roaring engines and spinning wheels, the roof-mounted searchlights exploring what lay ahead, the falling snow looking contrastingly peaceful as it was caught in the quick-moving beams. That was the first time I saw and heard Porsches in action, and I was impressed by their newness, uniqueness and effectiveness.

Yes, I knew then that a Porsche had all it took to make it a true sports car, and more. And it was accomplished in such clever ways; it was rear-engined, air-cooled and aerodynamic. Yes, the Porsche was unique, sensible and honest in every way. It not only matched the definition of a sports car, it exceeded it; a sports car should now also be economical, dependable and comfortable.

It was this concept that quickly earned Porsche a place at the top — a concept that, enthusiasts agree, captures the essence of a sports car.

Porsche's second-generation steering wheel, the first of its own design and introduced on the 1953 models, decorates a 1958 Speedster, right. Ivory color gave a distinctive look and two spokes allowed a perfect view of the instruments. The third generation, introduced in 1959, was inspired by emerging concern for safety; it was now concave, black and had three spokes. A horn ring was optional, as seen on a 1965 SC Cabriolet, left. A Les Lester wheel fit snugly in the 904 cockpit, above. Spokes were engine-turned, and a wood rim represented the classic racing look of the period.

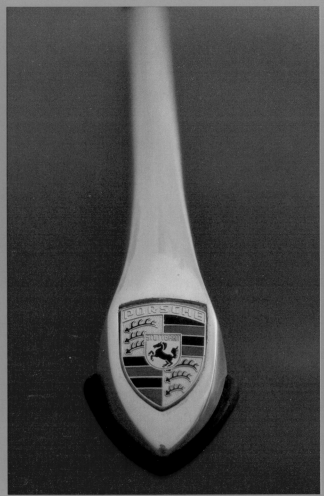

Early Porsches did not carry the coat of arms that has since become such a famous symbol. Not until 1953 did the crests of the state of Baden-Wuerttemberg and the city of Stuttgart supply the staghorns and the rampant horse for a design that from then on adorned every Porsche. Here it can be seen applied to a variety of surfaces: the chromed deck-lid handle of an A-series 356, the forged alloy wheel of a 924 Turbo and the shining paint surface of a 911. The scripts on the opposite page, found on the front fenders of two famous Porsche models, represent motoring pleasure in its purest form.

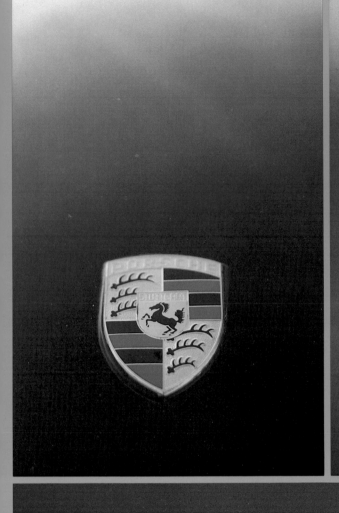

Primitive charm characterizes the cockpit of the 1955 550 Spyder, above, and the 1958 356 Speedster, left. The Spyder's low-cut, beautifully curved racing windshield and the Speedster's flimsy, minimal, no-frills side curtains recreate the open-air pleasures of the aviators and race drivers of the pioneer days. The interiors of the 1975 Carrera Targa, right, and the 1978 928, upper right, on the other hand, create a total contrast, expressing the ultimate in electronic refinement and upholstered luxury, encapsulating their occupants in an environment of relaxing comfort.

Shiny surfaces create the setting for this study of lights. The classic simplicity of the 356-series is represented by the close-up of a 1958 Speedster, above right; by the telephoto facia of a 1963 Carrera 2, far right; and by the wide-angle shot of a 1965 Cabriolet, above, its beehive lenses serving both as parking lights and blinkers. To the right, the much-developed 911 theme in the form of a 1979 930 Turbo, shows a beautiful solution to the same function. Far right, the exciting lines of a 928 is further proof that good design can prevail in the face of ever more complicating regulations.

Spoilers didn't spoil anything, although purists initially felt they did – visually. But, as with so many successful designs, the spoiler was based on a functional concept. Its first road-car application came on the 1973 Carrera RS, right, nicknamed "ducktail." It increased rear wheel grip by as much as 20 percent at top speed and also had several other positive effects on stability and handling. Further refinement came on the 1975 Carrera, above. Now enlarged, rubber-rimmed and horizontal, it was called a "whaletail." The final form is seen on the 1979 930 Turbo, left, with its large louvered area funneling air to the intercooler.

F irst used in 1952, Porsche's ventilated disc wheel was available painted, or as on the 1958 Speedster to the left, chromed. The hubcap was plain, but in 1959, with the arrival of the B-series, it carried the crest. Far left, Porsche's famous Fuchs forged alloy wheel, first available on the 911. On this 1973 Carrera RS, it was painted to match the Carrera script on the body side-panel. Above left, the cast alloy wheel of the 928 is not only distinctive, it also allows superb ventilation. Above, one of the best-looking wheel designs ever, Porsche's new forged alloy wheel, here fitted to a 1981 924 Turbo.

Four Porsche power units, all engineering masterpieces in their own rights, display their features on these pages. The basis was, of course, the development of Ferdinand Porsche's air-cooled push-rod engine for Volkswagen. In the 1958 1600 S Speedster, above, his engineering milestone produces 75 hp. Pictured to the right, the famous four-cam engine, designed by Ernst Fuhrmann. Here, mounted in the street version of the 1955 550 Spyder, it generated 110 hp. To the left, the ultimate development of the 911 power unit; the 1979 3.3-litre US-specification 930 Turbo has an output of 261 hp. To the far left, the latest creation from the Porsche engineers, the all-aluminum, liquid-cooled, fuel-injected V-8 of the 1978 928. It produces 219 hp, but was designed with much room for further development.

Chronology of Production

By Gene Babow

Ferdinand Anton Porsche, born in 1875 in Maffersdorf, Bohemia, was a genius. His detractors, may they rest in peace, said that he could scarcely draw a line. They forgot that genius extends to picking associates who can translate the ideas of the master.

He was wholeheartedly devoted to the pursuit of these ideas. It was not unusual for him to have a sandwich in his pocket, so that he could have a meal while working. He would often sleep for a brief moment in the most unexpected places. He valued time. He once said he intended to live to be one hundred because he felt he had so much left to do.

Ferdinand Porsche was a pioneer in the areas of front-wheel drive, four-wheel drive, four-wheel brakes, automatic transmissions, streamlining and mid-engined Grand Prix cars. With a flick of the pen he would design the Auto Union Grand Prix racer with sixteen cylinders, 545 hp and weighing 1,500 pounds; or the Volkswagen, using the same principles as the Auto Union, but placing them in a practical perspective.

He was full of dreams and worked hard for their realization. He was never satisfied with his designs; he always saw possibilities for their improvement, hence there were always changes in production. His view was: "Through sporting successes, we shall popularize our marque and thus we shall sell considerable numbers of vehicles." The Porsche as we know it today is living proof of the validity of this theory.

Porsche went to electro-technical school against his father's wishes. His father had wanted him to take over the family tin shop. At just eighteen, Porsche built a light-station in his father's home. At twenty-five, he had

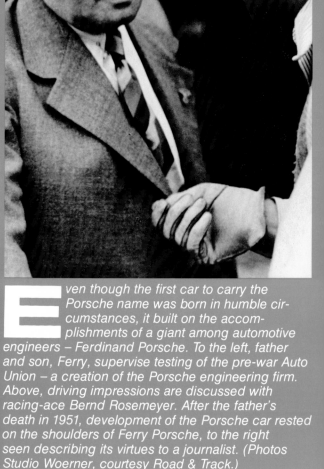

Even though the first car to carry the Porsche name was born in humble circumstances, it built on the accomplishments of a giant among automotive engineers – Ferdinand Porsche. To the left, father and son, Ferry, supervise testing of the pre-war Auto Union – a creation of the Porsche engineering firm. Above, driving impressions are discussed with racing-ace Bernd Rosemeyer. After the father's death in 1951, development of the Porsche car rested on the shoulders of Ferry Porsche, to the right seen describing its virtues to a journalist. (Photos Studio Woerner, courtesy Road & Track.)

already designed the front-wheel drive Lohner-Porsche. This vehicle had electric motors mounted in the front wheel hubs. Remember, the year was 1900! See if this sounds familiar: To prove the capabilities of the machine, he increased the power, applied a measure of streamlining and drove the Lohner-Porsche in record time up the Semmering Pass in Austria.

Thinking ahead, however, he saw the limitations in range and power of this type of vehicle. True, he tried the motors in the rear wheels, then in all four wheels and then, finally, he used a gas engine to provide energy to power the electric motors. But, he was now ready for new challenges. He left Lohner to start with Austro-Daimler. During this time he also won a competition event in another car he had designed — the Prince Henry model. Furthermore, he designed a small 1100 cc car called the Sascha, which won its class at the Targa Florio. One of his mechanics was a man who later gained prominence as Yugoslavia's premier and president, Marshall Tito. And one of his drivers was Alfred Neubauer. Later, Porsche would introduce Neubauer at Mercedes, where he would lead the competition department to numerous victories. Porsche himself also moved to Mercedes, where he was responsible for the fantastic S series Mercedes, including the S, SS, SSK and SSKL. After his sojourn with Mercedes he returned to Austria to work for Steyr; and later, he again joined Austro-Daimler.

The time is now 1930 and Porsche was tired of working for others. In a rented house on Kronenstrasse, in Stuttgart, Germany he started his own firm — offering consultation as well as complete designs of engines and vehicles. The House of Porsche began. The numbering system of Porsche designs started here. Not wanting his first client to think that it was the first design, Porsche started with number seven.

This first design, Type 7, was a small vehicle for the firm Wanderer. Type 12 was a Zündapp vehicle for the well-known motorcycle firm. Type 22 was the Grand Prix Auto Union. Type 60 was the Volkswagen. Type 82 was a jeep-like derivative of the VW, known as the Kubelwagen. Type 101 was the Tiger tank. Type 128 was the water-going VW, known as the Schwimmwagen. Type 356 — we'll get to that shortly.

Porche's associates in the new firm included his son Ferdinand Anton Porsche II, nicknamed Ferry; Erwin Komenda, who would execute the styling of the 356 as well as the 550 Spyder; Karl Rabe, chief designer and responsible for the torsion bar suspension; Franz Reimpeiss, who presented the first study of the platform design of the VW; Karl Frohlich, an expert in gearboxes; Josef Kales, aero-engine designer; Josef Mickl, a computer specialist before there were computers; and Joseph Zahradnick, specialist in steering and front suspension. A formidable list of talents.

While Porsche had long thought of a car bearing his name, the first attempt toward this goal was the car developed for the 1939 Berlin-Rome Race. The race never occurred because of World War II. Another design study, the Type 64, was meant to have been a sports-type vehicle on the VW theme. The state-owned VW firm, however, would have nothing to do with that kind of thinking. But, publicity gained through winning a race was a different matter. Porsche convinced the men in power that a VW-based car would be good for this purpose. This car, known as the Type 60K10, was built at Karosserie Reutter in Stuttgart.

One of the three Berlin-Rome cars built remained in Professor Porsche's possession. The car was purchased from him just after the war by Otto Mathé of Innsbruck, Austria. Porsche needed the money to start production of the Type 356. The prototype was built as a mid-engined car and based mostly on VW parts, so a contract with VW was needed at this time. The contract prevented Porsche from designing a competitor to the VW; a sizeable sum of money accompanied the agreement — this money also came in handy in the development of the Porsche sports car.

A small series of fifty cars were planned. They would be made in Gmünd, Austria. Based on the VW, but with modifications for the sporting aspect, the series would be made of aluminum. (Otto Mathé bought two of the Gmünd coupes; he still has them.) The acceptance of the Porsche was gratifying. A move back to Stuttgart was finally possible.

In Stuttgart, space was rented from Reutter. Tradition had to start someplace, and this was the place. Quality was to be first and foremost. The fit of the doors, hood and trunk required handwork to maintain a minimum space between the openings. The last digits of the car's serial number were stamped on each part. The surface of the body was also hand-finished. Zero flaws ensured quality. The car was assembled for fit, then disassembled for painting. All parts were painted at once, in an area which was surgically clean.

In 1951, Professor Porsche died, partially as a result of his war-related imprisonment in France. He did not live to be one hundred, and he still had many things to do. But his son, Ferry, carried on in a manner that the master would have been proud of.

By 1954, 5,000 of the Type 356 models had been made. The Porsche philosophy continued: The factory

*S*hape of things to come! Created for the 1939 Berlin-Rome race, this aerodynamic coupe introduced the concept that would later form the basis for the first Porsche. The war forced cancellation of the race, so the three cars built were never put to their true test. Of the three, one was wrecked during the war, another was vandalized by occupation forces, and the third still survives in the hands of Austrian race driver Otto Mathé who purchased it from Porsche right after the war and raced it very successfully. These pictures, by Gene Babow, show the way it looks today in Mathé's garage – still basically original.

raced cars but also encouraged private owners to race them. Class wins in races and rallies were now commonplace. Starting in 1951, Porsche won its class at Le Mans. Looking ahead, however, it was readily apparent that the 356 was too heavy and the VW-based four-cylinder push-rod engine was near its limit of development for racing use.

In Frankfurt, the family Glöckler raced a special lightweight Porsche. It did well. Erwin Komenda improved the styling and the Type 550 took shape. The new engine, Type 547, was designed almost totally by Dr. Ernst Fuhrmann. It was a four-cam, four-cylinder, air-cooled unit. It was right from the beginning. The initial goal of 100 hp/liter was achieved just a few years later. Fuhrmann kept the outside dimensions of the engine similar to the push-rod one. It was obvious it was meant for the street as well as for the track.

Perhaps this is a good time to go into nomenclature, especially as it relates to the Type 356. The Stuttgart production Porsche 356 lasted from 1950-1965. There were four major subspecies: the 356, from 1950-1955; the 356A, from 1956-1959; the 356B, from 1960-1963; the 356C from 1964-1965. These are considered model years. In true Porsche tradition, continual changes abounded, year by year.

No complications should arise in trying to comprehend the different body styles. True, they transgressed the subspecies, but the two basic ones were constant; the coupe was always available, from 1950-1965, as was the cabriolet — a fancy convertible with roll-up windows, a padded top and headliner.

In 1952 and 1953, the America Roadster was produced in limited numbers by Heuer Body Works in Weiden. It was the Type 540. Only sixteen were made before another roadster, which it inspired, made its entrance — the Speedster.

Max Hoffman, the early distributor for Porsche in the United States, wanted an inexpensive leader to sell. A special series called the America (not to be confused with the Type 540 roadster, same name) coupe and cabriolet was sold. It had no identification on the outside and is known by very few. It was stripped of the rear seat and other niceties and sold for about $3,300. By late 1954, the name was changed to "Continental." Although not a catalog model from the factory, magazine ads from Hoffman show this model. Some cars even had the name on the front fenders. A threatened law suit from Ford Motor Company, because they were planning to reintroduce the Continental MK II, caused a third name, "European," to be used. By 1956, model designation reverted to simply 1600 and 1600Super within the 356A Series.

Probably the most recognized early Porsche, the Speedster, was introduced in 1954 and continued into 1959. The Convertible D (for Drauz, the coachbuilder) was a 1959 model only, carrying the Speedster body, but now with a higher windshield and roll-up windows. By now, the demand for Porsches outstripped the capacity of Reutter to build them. Karmann of Osnabruk was called on to supplement the production. In 1960, with the introduction of the B-Series, the D became the Roadster. In 1961, production of that Roadster shifted to D'Ieteren Fréres in Belgium. Karmann produced a notchback coupe that looked like the cabriolet with a hardtop, called simply the Karmann coupe.

The complication in nomenclature was caused by the various displacements of the engines. Rounded-off displacement numbers identified the engines. The push-rod engine of 1950 displaced 1086 cc; it was called the 1100, and so on. There were engines of 1300, 1500 and 1600 designations. Again in true Porsche tradition, there was a more powerful S designation in the 1300, 1500 and 1600 types. In 1961, an even more powerful engine was introduced — it was called the Super 90. It put out 90 DIN hp. From 1955 on the four-cam engines were also used in the 356 series and they were then usually called Carreras. They displaced from 1500 to 2000 cc.

Up until the 356C series, nomenclature was simple. For instance, you might have a 1961 356B with a normal 1600 engine in a coupe. In 1964, the normal engine was dropped and the 1600S engine would be designated the 356C and the Super 90 engine would be known as the 356SC. Either could be had in the coupe or cabriolet. Now, that wasn't hard, was it?

Now for the curve ball — the four-cam-engined cars: 1500GS, GS/GT, Carrera 2, 2000GS/GT and 904. These were all road and race cars of the Type 356, (except for the 904) powered by the Fuhrmann four-cam engine. This fabulous engine, a veritable giant-killer, would power Porsche road and race cars for a decade in rapid fashion. Even today, they power the vintage racers in winning style. In sizes from 1100 cc to 2000 cc, they made a racing name of Porsche.

Nomenclature aside, the Porsche was meant to be driven. It brought a new dimension to sports car driving. The car challenged the driver to join forces and operate as one. The famous auto writer, Ken Purdy, said, "You almost never see a bored Porsche driver." The balance of this car was something new — power, handling and brakes complemented each other. Steering was light and quick, gearbox was smooth with

Porsche Number One saw light in 1948. These pictures were taken in a converted sawmill in Gmünd, Austria, temporary home of the Porsche engineering firm. Top, the wooden buck used to check the fit of the hand-hammered body panels. Above, workmen attending to details of the still unpainted body. Left, the engine was a Volkswagen, although it now sported dual carburetors and modified cylinder heads. Right bottom, Porsche Number One, a roadster, resting behind Porsche Number Two, a coupe, its front shown above. (Photographs by Porsche Werkfoto, courtesy Ray Stewart.)

hand-picked ratios and the car could slice through holes that didn't exist for other cars. Even the 1600 normal could go point-to-point with a 300 hp opponent and often be there first. The more curves, the more likely it was that it would be first. More important, the driver would be wearing a big smile and be relaxed enough to do it again.

A little out of order, the Type 904 is included here. It still had the four-cam engine. It was both a road and race car. Different power was available for each owner option. To reduce weight, a fiberglass body was utilized that was made by Heinkel, the aircraft manufacturer. The frame was box steel, to which the body was bolted and bonded. The car was designed by Ferdinand Porsche III, also known as Butzi.

Around 1960, a new touring car was being formulated. It would be a continuation of the Type 356, but faster and roomier. The engine, designated Type 901, would be a six-cylinder, air-cooled unit, displacing two liters and producing 130 DIN hp at 6200 rpm. The new model was introduced at the Frankfurt Auto Show in 1963. The body was styled by Butzi Porsche. Because a French automaker held the rights to all three-digit numbers with a zero in the middle, the new model identification had to be changed from 901 to 911. Deliveries of the new car started in late 1964. In 1965, the old four-cylinder engine was installed in a lower-priced version called the 912.

Back to nomenclature. The 912 stayed as the 912 from 1965-1969. The 911 transversed an alphabet soup of letters that still continues. The 911 added an S in 1967. Right, more power and the new alloy wheels by Fuchs! In 1968, the S was joined by the letters T and L. T was for touring, the lower-priced 911; L was for luxury, replacing the S in the United States because of emission regulations. In 1969, the L was dropped and replaced by an E, for Einspritzung or fuel injection. The S was reinstated in the United States. There was also an R, but that was a lightweight racing model in 1968. The T, E and S continued until 1973. In 1974, the T was dropped completely. The E became the lower-priced model and reverted to the plain 911.

A small series of fast cars were made in 1973, and were only available in Europe, where they were called the Carrera RS. In 1974, the engine was toned down and became the Carrera, now available in the United States. In 1975, the plain 911 was dropped, and the 911S and Carrera remained. In 1975, a 25th Anniversary model of the 911 was sold. These 750 special silver cars carried a numbered plaque with Ferry Porsche's signature. Next year, the Carrera was turbocharged and became the 930. The designation 912E appeared — it was a 911 body with the Type IV VW engine. It covered the period from the end of the 914 until introduction of the 924. In 1978, the S designation was dropped and became the 911SC.

The 911 is still going strong after eighteen years. The design is still in style and time has not affected the looks of the car. Flares on the fenders and the choice of either coupe or Targa still satisfies owners in spite of the fact that the 1964 price of $6,000 has increased to more than $30,000, for various and sundry reasons.

Backtracking a little, the mid-engined 914 was introduced as a 1970 model. The VW 1700 cc engine was used. The body was manufactured by Karmann. The introductory price in the United States was $3,595. The 914/6 was completed at the Porsche factory and outfitted with the 1969 911T engine, displacing 2000 cc. The 911 for 1970 displaced 2200 cc. The 914/6 was dropped in 1972 and replaced in 1973 by the 914/2.0, which had a more powerful four-cylinder engine than that of the original 914 version. The 914 lasted until 1976.

The 914 was as much a Porsche as was the Type 356. What's wrong with using VW parts? Many manufacturers wish they could. The handling of the 914 was delightful. The Targa-type roof and the two trunks were popular. A derivative of the 914, the 916, was planned. It would have the 2.4-liter 911 engine, and be quite expensive. The latter stopped production at just a handful. It could also have become too much of a competitor to the 911, which it would easily have surpassed in handling and performance.

Let's return to the Turbo. The 930 Turbo has to be the ultimate Porsche. It signifies all that Professor Porsche could have foreseen, except that he would probably have improvements already in motion and it would still be sold in the United States — it was not after 1979.

What would Professor Porsche have said about the 924 and 928? Both are complete turn-arounds for Porsche. They are liquid-cooled and front-engined.

In reference to the 924, he would be happy that in four years, more than 100,000 have been sold. Would he have changed anything on the car? He did design a similar trans-axle for Mercedes; it was used in the Mercedes Grand Prix cars in the thirties.

The 928 would probably be in his garage, next to the 930 Turbo. Both would be used. He would appreciate the luxury of the 928. It may be the best Porsche yet. Following Porsche tradition, there is now a 928S. He would appreciate that model and also have something in mind for future development. He would be disenchanted with the sales of the 928 and the way it is

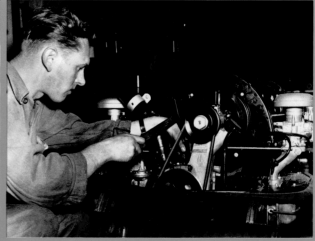

Now finally back in Stuttgart, where Porsche's engineering firm had been located before the war, 1950 saw the beginning of serious production of the Porsche car. Reutter, the coachbuilder, made a small area available to Porsche in its Zuffenhausen facility and also supplied bodies, above and left. Above, the engine receives final touches. Now could also begin all the activities necessary to launch a new make: Porsche tested on the Autobahn, Porsche taking part in Concours d'Elegance, Porsche posed in snow, Porsche competing in races. (Photos by Studio Woerner, courtesy Road & Track.)

advertised. He would have been pushing hard for a competition version to get sales rolling.

He would look at Dr. Ing. h. c. F. Porsche AG and be proud. The factory in the outskirts of Stuttgart/Zuffenhausen has grown immensely from the rented space at Reutter's. He would note that Reutter had been taken over by Porsche in the early sixties. (Speaking of Reutter, the firm now builds seats for Porsche and other companies under the name Recaro. Recaro is actually an anacronym taken from the first two letters of Reutter and letters from Karosserie.)

Financially, the small firm of Porsche has not had one year of red ink; it has always been in the black. In effect, the racing was paid for by the resulting increase in sales. More black ink came, and comes, from designing and consulting for outside firms. In 1947, after the war, Porsche had as much money coming in from this source as it had before the war started.

This black ink is all the more amazing when you look at the history of automobile manufacturers. Of the 5,000 makes started over the almost one hundred years of automobile production, only a handful still survive. Even this handful is not secure, some are teetering now. Try to name some manufacturers who have started since 1948 and are still in business. It is much easier to name those who have failed since 1948.

The future of current road cars from Porsche has to be speculative. However, it is said by Porsche officials that the 911 series will last as long as buyers will purchase them. This could be changed by increased smog requirements, especially in the United States.

The 924 will remain, but the engine will probably be all Porsche. At Le Mans this year (1981) a 924 took seventh place overall. It was powered by the 2.5 liter half of the 928 engine. It will be called the Porsche 944. The 928 will stay as is. The more powerful 928S will not meet United States smog regulations.

More than 500,000 Porsches have been made. It is still a small company; remember, Chevy can produce that many in six months, but they are just Chevys.

When Dr. Ernst Fuhrmann was president of Porsche, he said, "The president of Volkswagen, a big firm, drives a Volkswagen; the president of Opel, a big firm, drives an Opel; I am president of Porsche, a small firm, I drive a Porsche 928S."

May Porsche always stay that way. They build a car that demands to be driven hard; a car that is conceived with controls at the fingertips, built to last with a minimum of servicing, gets a respectable number of miles per gallon and still performs as you would expect a sports car to perform.

550 SPYDER

Long Live The Spyders!

Like an individual, an automobile also has a destiny. And the two are often intertwined. Sometimes, at best, they are destined to become loved, pampered and treated with respect. Other times, most of the time, they are destined to just roll along, without any special significance, ending up in some forgotten place. And sometimes they are headed straight for disaster, destined for a short, dramatic life, ending in tragedy.

I look across the vast, gold-colored territory that surrounds me. To the north, to the south, to the east, there is not a house to be seen, not a tree, not a bush. The vastness begins at the roadside where I stand, expands uninterrupted, rolls gently along the contours of the valley floor, rises into hills, covers them with gold, monotonous gold, and continues on until it meets blue sky, monotonous blue.

To the east, the dark gray of a road, thin in the beginning, like a string, cuts through the hills and widens gradually as it runs on across the valley. To the northeast, another road, another string, widens, runs on, straight as a cutting-edge, finally meeting up with that first road, exactly where I stand. The two roads, joined in one, continues behind me, curves, passes a group of buildings, and travels on westbound.

There is an eerie stillness here. Nothing moves. Not even the cows seem to move, grazing in the distance, looking like black dots sprinkled among the gold. And there is an eerie silence. It makes me aware of what once took place here. I bend down by the roadside, looking for crumbled pieces of aluminum.

Suddenly, the silence is broken by the distant sound of an engine. As it nears, I can hear that it comes from a truck. But on that day, September 30, 1955, it was not a Mack, nor was it a Kenworth approaching the point where the two roads meet. No, on that day, long ago, it was a Porsche 550 Spyder. Its silver-colored, low-slung, aerodymanic body penetrated the air like a bullet, shooting toward that crucial intersection with a speed of eighty-five miles an hour. Its young, famous-faced driver, sunglasses shielding his eyes, speed-

The 550 Spyder was inspired by a series of Porsche-powered cars built and raced by Walter Glöckler as early as 1950. To the left, the first of these, driven by Heinz Brendel, is on its way to a class win in the 1952 Eifelrennen. Above, Hans Herrmann and Herbert Linge, in the cockpit of one of the prototype Spyders, return from a practice run at the factory. They later drove the same car to a class win in the 1954 Mille Miglia. Johnny von Neumann successfully campaigned another prototype in the United States. Pictured to the upper right, he is preparing for a start in Bakersfield. The photographs in the lower right show two production version Spyders, one sporting a plexiglas bubble at Hockenheim, the other being guided through a curve by German driver Theo Helfrich.

wind tugging at his hair, a content smile curving his lips, suddenly noticed a black Ford, facing him, slowing down, preparing to turn onto the road running in a northeasterly direction.

The famous-faced young driver expected the Ford to stop before it turned. Normally it would have. By law it should have. But on that day, it did not stop, and then, realizing it was his moment of truth, he saw that it was too late to correct his speed and direction.

The heavy, strong-built Ford caught the light, thin-skinned race car exactly at the point where the driver sat. The Porsche skidded on, came to a rest up against a fence, a twisted heap of aluminum, the passenger thrown clear, the driver's legs caught between steering wheel and pedals, his body hanging out across the door, his neck broken.

James Dean, twenty-four, actor, race driver, was fatally injured, and later, dead in the ambulance.

I walk over to my car, parked by the roadside. On the way back I again look for crumbled aluminum pieces, ridiculous, of course, since every bit and piece must long since have disappeared. I drive the short distance to the buildings. They turn out to be a village by the name of Cholame, population sixty-five, barely visible on my California map. I stop for gas.

Sure, Glen, the manager of the station, remembers. He was playing basketball over by the school when it happened. Later, that same evening, he saw the wreck himself. It was sitting there in front of the garage. Right there, Glen points.

Some time after the accident, the engine was sold and installed in another race car. The transmission was also sold. The body was obtained by the traffic safety people who displayed it all over the country to show what happens when you drive too fast. The last time the wreck was seen it was on a train back from Florida. When the train arrived at its destination, the wreck was not on it. Some say it was stolen and cut up in small pieces, sold as souvenirs.

James Dean's Spyder was a mid-run chassis number of the first series. All in all there were about two hundred built. Of these, only ninety were of the first series. This was the destiny of one of them.

Chassis number 061 had a different destiny. It was delivered on September 2, 1955, in Butte, Montana, about the same time as James Dean took possession of his Spyder. It is known that 061 was raced extensively. It was seen on tracks all over the Pacific Northwest. When the original four-cam engine blew, a Corvair engine was installed. Later a supercharged

(continued on overleaf)

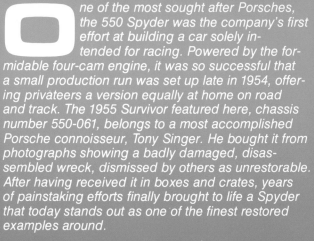

One of the most sought after Porsches, the 550 Spyder was the company's first effort at building a car solely intended for racing. Powered by the formidable four-cam engine, it was so successful that a small production run was set up late in 1954, offering privateers a version equally at home on road and track. The 1955 Survivor featured here, chassis number 550-061, belongs to a most accomplished Porsche connoisseur, Tony Singer. He bought it from photographs showing a badly damaged, disassembled wreck, dismissed by others as unrestorable. After having received it in boxes and crates, years of painstaking efforts finally brought to life a Spyder that today stands out as one of the finest restored examples around.

engine was fitted. The car went through a succession of eight owners, all adding to it and subtracting from it, until it finally was left sitting in the corner of a garage, the original engine and transmission in boxes, the body panels apart and demolished, separated from the frame, dry-rotting, wasting away. The owner had at first thought it would be possible to restore it but he finally gave up on that idea and decided to sell it. His ad appeared in Auto Week.

Tony Singer of Long Island, New York, was turned into a Porsche enthusiast after he had bought a 1963 Super 90 in 1971. By 1974 he also owned a 904 and happened to see a red Spyder in a showroom on Long Island. It was for sale. Until then he had been unaware that such a Porsche existed. Now, seeing it, discovering it, he thought the beautiful styling and the honest engineering made it the ultimate Porsche. He decided to sell the 904, but by then, the Spyder was gone. Tony Singer did not give up. About a year later he found an ad in Auto Week.

It took another year before he was able to close the deal and take delivery of 061. At that time he had still only seen photographs of it. And they had not looked encouraging. Everyone he had showed them to had thought it would be next to impossible to restore it. No one had ever put a Spyder body back on its frame since it was done at the factory more than twenty years earlier. But Tony Singer did not give up.

He assigned the restoration to Grand Prix SSR of Setauket, New York. Tony Dutton was responsible for the day-to-day work. Tony Singer was keeping himself occupied with research for authenticity and acquisition of missing parts. He even went out and bought two more Spyders, chassis numbers 059 and 089, so they could be studied for clues of how the 550 originally was put together. When it was found that they were not fully authentic, he managed to borrow 090, the last one built and still perfectly unaltered.

After 2,300 man-hours and two-and-a-half years, the Spyder finally stood ready for its premier showing at the 1978 Porsche Parade in Aspen, Colorado. It was awarded the coveted Judges Choice.

The Stradivarius violin, a masterpiece, is now on it's third century. Its course of destiny has been varied. The Porsche Spyder, another masterpiece, is only going on its fourth decade. No one knows what destiny has in store. We know Tony Singer's is in good hands. And who knows, preposterously, of course, maybe right now someone is quietly buying up all the small pieces of James Dean's Spyder, attempting to put it all back together. Who knows?

Pictured to the left, top, a line-up of production version 550 Spyders. These are works-prepared cars with the one closest to the camera possibly a Le Mans competitor. Bottom, the Spyder and the Jagdwagen, both in limited production, shared the same space at the Porsche factory. Above, top, one of the photographs of chassis number 061 that Tony Singer saw before he bought it. The picture clearly shows the deplorable state of the car. Bottom, Tony's Spyder takes shape in the workshop at Grand Prix SSR. To the right, top, the tubular ladder-type frame of the production version 550. Bottom, 550A Spyders under construction at the Weidenhausen coachworks in Frankfurt in 1956. Note the new space-type frame.

356A SPEEDSTER

Top Down and Flat Out!

We've just raised the top on Rudy Binkele's Speedster, parked outside his home in the hillside outskirts of San Luis Obispo. It's a very simple operation to raise that top. And it looks very good with those two bows set far back, pushing up like on a tent, the canvas tight like a drumskin, and with that long, unsuspended stretch of canvas falling off dramatically to meet with that super-low windshield.

"I've noticed that people look with more excitement at the Speedster when the top is up!" Rudy says. "It must be because it's so outrageously low. Another reason is that they can't see the driver. All they can see is a shoulder and a pair of hands holding the steering wheel. Unless you lean forward, you've no vision at all to the sides, especially if you're six-foot-three, like I am. No vision at all!"

"I guess that top is just for looking at!" I say.

"Yes, that's about all it's good for. You don't really need it when you drive in the rain. It shoots right over your head anyway."

"You have to keep on driving forever." I say. "But you can't do that when you're held up by a red light. Or when you get the gate at a railroad crossing, or when you've the road blocked by cattle."

"That's when you reach behind the seats and pull the top up. You don't fasten it because you want to let it down again as soon as you're ready to go!"

"You don't happen to have a yardstick or something else to measure with, do you?" I ask. "I'd like to see how low that windshield actually is. In inches!"

"I'll go get something!" Rudy says and walks off toward the house, turning his head, glancing at the Speedster, sitting there, looking fat and round.

"Looks like a tank!" he says and disappears.

When Rudy Binkele first saw a Speedster — that was in Santa Barbara in the mid-fifties — he thought it was the ugliest thing he had ever seen. Compared to his own Chevy it was, of course, strange looking. But after he had seen what the Speedster could do on a racetrack, he was completely sold.

The unique photographs on these pages were taken in the mid-Fifties. At this point, Porsche employed around six hundred workers, who turned out an average of seventeen cars a day. Pictured above, a portion of the assembly hall; a Speedster body is hanging from its travers in the foreground, a worker is in the process of lining up brake drums, and mufflers are being brought up on a cart. Pictured to the left, the chassis is being manufactured with the help of a special jig. To the right, top, a Speedster body, painted and trimmed, is ready to be mated to its chassis. To the right, bottom, a line-up of half-finished bodies, Speedsters in the foreground, Coupes in the background.

It would take almost twenty-five years and eight different Porsches before he finally got this Speedster. He traded his 1959 RSK Spyder to get it. The RSK had been drastically modified. It had eight-inch tires and flared fenders and a 912 engine instead of the original four-cam. He had driven it in club-level competition and had also shown it successfully, but with his restaurant business taking more and more time, the RSK ended up collecting dust. He found himself looking for a car he could drive anytime, anywhere — an exciting road-machine like the Speedster. The one he got was perfectly restored to original specifications. It was so good, in fact, that he won several firsts in shows. But that wasn't what he really had in mind for it. You can't have a Speedster sitting there, just to look at. So nowadays, he drives it often and hard on a loop of his favorite back-country roads.

Rudy drove the loop just this morning. I was a passenger. The California sun was already so hot, in spite of the speed-wind, that we had to get back to the house for something to drink. Soon its my turn to take the Speedster out on the loop.

While I'm waiting for Rudy I open the lid to the engine compartment. It's all so simple and clean and understandable in there. There's the generator. There are the carburetors. There's the oil filter. And so on. It's almost simple enough for me to think that I could do some work on it myself. Maybe.

I walk around to the front lid and open it. The battery, the spare wheel and the jack are located all the way up front — to counteract the weight of the engine in the rear. The fuel tank is set up against the back of the dashboard. In front of it is a space, about fourteen inches deep. A pouch, holding the side-curtains, fits precisely in that space. I take them out and place them on the car, fitting the pins in their holes, and pulling down the leather straps over the small pins on the inside of the door. It gives me a strange sensation, like preparing for a mission of some kind.

Rudy comes back with a seamstress' measuring tape dangling from around his neck, looking like a tailor, and looking like a bartender too, with a glass of Coke and ice in each hand. Between sips, I measure the windshield. Vertically, the area of vision is nine inches. I measure the side-curtains too. The vision area is only six inches.

"Not to look through. To look at!" I say.

I'm behind the steering wheel now. It was sixteen inches across, by the way. Rudy sits in the passenger seat, looking calmer than he probably is. We're ac-

(continued on overleaf)

From any angle, the Speedster is a most appealing and exciting design, as unique today as it was when introduced in 1954. Its round, slippery forms were developed without the aid of a wind tunnel, and it is a credit to stylist Erwin Komenda's concepts. Later testing has proven the original 356 shape to be one of the most aerodynamically efficient designs. The early-morning, fog-swept beach proves as fitting a location for this 1958 1600 S Speedster, chassis number 84300, and its enthusiast-owner Rudy Binkele, as their normal habitats of country roads, racetracks and car shows.

celerating through the gears now, the stick feeling loose and flimsy, just as I had expected, remembering my experiences with Volkswagens, and needing long movements, the speed-wind flowing noisily across the top of the windshield, bugs splashing onto it. The car is doing close to eighty now, in fourth, the road straight but narrow, dropping off, and ahead, curving sharply to the left.

"Don't let up yet!" I hear Rudy shouting over the engine, busy sounding in its characteristic hammering, whining, rushing way. "You don't have to brake until you hit that 25-mph sign up there. Now! Shift!"

I down-shift to third, brake, and nudge the car carefully over to the left, cutting grass, a little on edge because I've heard stories about how easy the backend goes; but the Speedster sticks to the road like it was glued, and I steer it back to the right and accelerate, throwing it in fourth, the road going slightly uphill now, and turning to the right further ahead. I relax for a moment, feeling how tightly the seat holds me. I push back in it, realizing then how upright the driver sits compared to today's lay-down racing position.

"Don't let up!" I hear Rudy shout again. "That's another 60-mph curve up there! Go close to the telephone pole on the right. But don't go too close!"

I down-shift and go through that one too. It's a repeat of the first. The road is running uphill now. I keep it in third until I reach the crest, then accelerate and put it in fourth, calmly pressing the gas pedal to the floor. The road is straight, running downhill, and bumpy, and I feel the suspension working. It's not as stiff as I had expected. In fact, it's not stiff at all. The speed is increasing now, the wind becoming aggressive, the needle closing up on one hundred. Golden hills are rushing by on both sides, and barbed wire fences, and cows and horses and sheep, and telephone poles, and Keep-Out signs, and No-Hunting-Posted signs, and windmills, and mailboxes, and hay freshly cut, and hay uncut. I feel in control. The cockpit is the center of it all. Just in front of me I see the top of the low curving windshield, and the curving dashboard, so simple and beautiful, and beyond it the curving hood and fenders, it all being curvy and round and sensuous; behind me, the engine is working hard and enjoying it, enjoying it like a racehorse stretching out on the straightaway to win.

"Now you know why they call it a Speedster!" I hear Rudy shouting, and turning my head quickly I see him smiling, calm as ever. He can't be as calm as he looks, I think to myself. I decide to keep that pedal nailed to the floor for as long as I can . . .

Pictured in this spread are various 356-series dashboards. Above, a 1950 Cabriolet. It used the Petra steering wheel, and did not yet have a crest on its horn button. Left, a Coupe from the same period. The 1951 photograph focuses on the reclining passenger seat. To the near right, top, a 1953 model, now sporting both a new steering wheel and a crest. Notice also the eye-lids above the two large gauges. Center, a 1954 Speedster. It has two large dials and a small center-mounted one. Later models had three of equal size. Bottom, the dash of an A-series Coupe. Three equally-sized gauges is now the style. Far right, top, the interior of a B-series Coupe with a new steering wheel, but basically the same layout. Bottom, the B-series Roadster. (Photos courtesy Road & Track).

356B CARRERA 2

Carrera Nostalgia

You can talk Porsche anywhere. Al Hansen and I talk Porsche as we park his Carrera 2 in front of the Bella Union Saloon in Jacksonville on this slow-paced, off-work, sun-bright Saturday morning. First time we've seen the sun in two months, Al says. Jacksonville was once the capitol of Oregon. It was a center of gold mining, but it didn't die like so many other gold-rush towns. It lived on, thanks to its gold. Even during the depression, they lived off of the gold they dug out from tunnels under their houses. Al tells me all this. But we're really talking Porsche.

We open the doors to the Saloon and walk across the planks that make you think you see bullet holes in them from all the gunfights you imagine must have taken place in here. We pick a window table so we can keep an eye on Al's Carrera. Al orders the omelette with onions and cheese. I know it's still breakfast, Miss, but I must have the warm German sausage, lovingly simmered in dark beer, as the menu reads, and served with sauerkraut. I must, Miss. Goes with our Porsche talk, I say.

You know, Al says, the young-generation Porsche enthusiasts, they probably have no idea where the Carrera name comes from, do they? They probably think the Porsche sales people grabbed it from out of thin air, like Detroit would do. Don't you think? But you and I know that it comes from one of the most fantastic road races ever put on. Carrera Panamericana, I say. Really has a ring to it, doesn't it?

Wasn't it first run in 1950, I ask? Yes, I think an Olds won it that year. The Mexicans put the race on to promote their new Panamerican Highway, you know. It started just south of El Paso on the United States border and ran all the way to the Guatemalan border. But there were no Porsches in it that first year.

I think the first time was 1953, wasn't it? I don't think any Porsches ran it in 1951. But in 1952, one came in eighth. And in 1953, two Guatemalans ran the two 550 prototypes. I know that. One broke down, but the other won its class. At the end there were only two

In this spread the camera has captured for posterity some of the activities of those rare Gmünd Coupes. In the two photographs at the top of this page, Johnny von Neumann, California Porsche pioneer, rounds the hay bales during a race at Pebble Beach. Later, the same car was raced with its roof cut off. Above, a picturesque scene from the 1951 record-run at Monthlery. Wearing a mustache and scarf is Porsche's competition boss, Huschke von Hanstein. To the left, the Coupe is frozen by the flash during the evening portion of the run. The first Porsche victory at Le Mans came in 1951; Veuillet and Mouche drove their Coupe to a class win. Right, top, their #46 car gets some well-earned juice. Bottom, the same drivers repeated their Le Mans win the following year. (Photos courtesy Road & Track and Gene Babow.)

cars left in the class. The other was a stock 356.

But, of course, they didn't have the four-cammer in those cars, did they? No, they first used the four-cammer in 1954, when Hans Herrmann won the class and placed third overall. Yes, that was the last year of the race and the year of the big Porsche win. Just think about that. At the finish, after five days of flat-out racing, the one-and-a-half-liter Porsche was still right up there among those big four-and-a-half- and five-liter Ferraris. Just think about that. Yes, 1954 was the year of Porsche's big Carrera win. The next year, in 1955, they put the four-cammer in the 356 body and called it Carrera.

1955, I think to myself, chewing on the natural casing of those German sausages while Al is working on the last of his omelette, yes, 1955 was a good year. I saw Hammarlund win at Skarpnack that year, in Sweden, on that monotonous, curve-straightaway-curve-straightaway airport circuit outside Stockholm. Yes, I can still see him coming up on that hairpin turn in his silver Carrera, braking for all he's worth, tires smoking, down-shifting quickly, the four-cammer rumbling and coughing and spitting fire, the whole car tilting heavily on its springs as it rounds the corner, the right side of the front skirt almost scraping the track, the tires screaming, and then, that slippery silver shape shooting out of the turn, passing all the other cars, accelerating down the straightaway, now with that fully open, fully unleashed four-cammer sound loud and throaty, and every time he's shifting, the backend of that low-slung body sinking even lower, the rear wheels flexing wide, a puff of blue smoke shooting out from that fat exhaust pipe, and finally, the Carrera getting smaller and smaller while the other cars are still in second gear. Yes, 1955 was a good year.

Say, Al, your Carrera is a 1963, right? Any racing history? Yes, it was raced in France, Al says. The owner's manual is in French. Doesn't do me any good because I can't read it, but it shows that the car was delivered in France. Also, the speedometer is in kilometers. From France the car went to Germany. Frank Hunt of Minneapolis brought it over and restored it. Did a very good job.

I look out through the window at the Carrera 2. It looks just like a regular B-series coupe, doesn't it, I say, except for that louvered skirt below the rear bumper. Right, Al says, and minus the grilles over the openings below the headlights. The Carrera 2 has oil coolers there, and they need all the ventilation they can get. But let's have a ride in it now, Al says. Yes, (continued on overleaf)

Here is what the uninitiated would call a typical early Porsche, but it's actually not the earliest style. The B- and C-series coupes, with their raised bumpers, lights and fenders, differed slightly from the original 356. The Survivor featured here, chassis number 122214, belonging to restorer and collector Al Hansen, also differs in another important way. As an expert would recognize, the lack of horn grills below the headlights shows that it is a 2000 GS Carrera 2. It has the potent four-cam engine on board, capable of catapulting this B-series 1963 classic from 0-60 in less than nine seconds, thus making it the fastest of all 356-series road Porsches.

let's I say. I'm ready for it. Thank you, Miss. Those German sausages sure worked wonders for our conversation. Thank you very much, Miss.

Al wants me to drive. I don't mind. Be sure to keep the revs up, he says, or else the plugs will foul. The four-cammer is famous for that. Keep it over twenty-five hundred to be on the safe side. But don't run it up above four thousand. It's still being run in.

When that like-nothing-else sound starts pouring out through the dual pipes, even though it's muffled, sidewalk car enthusiasts turn their heads. A Porsche? Doesn't sound like one. Is it really? I keep the revs up, find the catching point of the clutch, let it out, and get off and away in a fairly decent fashion, keeping the revs up at the proper level. That low, guttural note comes willingly from somewhere deep inside.

You don't want to have to clean the plugs on this one, I say, talking louder now. They are pretty hard to get to, aren't they? You bet, Al says, shaking his head, smiling, looking like he knows from experience. It's a very complicated engine from whatever way you look at it. It's difficult to work on unless you really know what you're doing. But it's beautiful and unique.

I have the open road ahead of me now. I run it up to four thousand in second, then shift to third, run it up to four thousand again, and let it float there. I'm feeling the beauty of it now. I give it more foot, feeling the car surging forward, hearing the sound opening up, and then, as the four-cammer reaches fifty-two hundred, sensing a vibration of power spreading through the floor and seat, reaching for my spine, and I know that's the way it should be.

Yes, Al says with a forgiving smile as I take my foot off and let the tach needle sink to four thousand, yes, that four-cammer sure is a beautiful machine. You should see the way the parts are made. Hand finished. Hand assembled. You should understand how everything works and why. What I know about the German people I have learned from Porsches; solid values, sound thinking and planning.

We cruise comfortably fast now, on a narrow road, curving in and out between fields and farms, mountains on both sides. Applegate Valley, Al says. You know what I like about old Porsches? I like that they are old. And I like that in spite of the fact that they are old they are still modern, he says. Yes, that's a very fine analysis, I say, as I down-shift, preparing for a hairpin curve, going in fast, keeping the revs correct, braking now. Yes, a very fine analysis.

You can talk Porsche anywhere, but it's especially good in an old Carrera.

The various Porsche Coupe models is the subject of this picture spread. On the opposite page, first column, top to bottom, the Gmünd model is first. Notice its peaked roof and high windshield. Next, the 1950 model with its split windshield. Next, the 1951 model which had a solid windshield, but retained the crease. On this page, above, the A-series. It now had the bumper separate from its body, and in this case, over-riders for the United States market. Back to the opposite page, second column, first, an A-series with detachable hardtop. Next, a photograph showing the effect of the 1959 restyling; an A to the right, and a B to the left. Finally, the Karmann Coupe. To the left, the Roto Hoist, conceived and manufactured by Al Hansen of Medford, Oregon. (Photos courtesy Road & Track.)

356 SC CABRIOLET

A Topless Review

Somewhere in Denver, there's a one-story brick building. There's no sign above the door, and there's nothing interesting about the outside of it. On the inside, is where it gets interesting. Bill Jackson keeps his Porsche collection in this building. Lined up along the walls are rows of cars, all under covers.

It's interesting just to guess what's hiding beneath those covers. But you have to know your models well, because there are things you may never have heard of. What about a Schwimmwagen? Or a Jagdwagen? Or a Porsche marine engine?

How about this one? I see familiar fender forms and part of an air dam below the cover. An RSR? Yes. One of the early Peter Gregg cars. And this? Another RSR. Yes. One of the three Martini prototype cars. Raced by the factory in 1973 and 1974. How did you ever manage to get that one? Bought it directly from them, Bill says without blinking.

This one should be easy, Bill says smiling, uncovering the 1965 SC Cabriolet I've come to photograph. Freshly polished and detailed, its champagne lacquer is shining, its black interior spotless. Lynne, my girlfriend, and I, Bill says, drove it to the Porsche Parade in Seattle. It's probably the best all-around Porsche you can own. It's quick. It handles well. It's economical. It's comfortable. And it's an open car! But the top is padded so it stays warm in the winter. And — it has the classic Porsche look!

It takes an hour to complete the tour. By then Bill is called away to other duties. I'll try to be back by three, he says. We'll shoot it at Red Rocks, all right? Perfect, I say, but don't rush! I knew I would find enough in the sanctuary to keep me occupied even if he should happen to be gone for a month.

The sanctuary is a suite of two rooms built within another large room in Bill Jackson's building. The literature collection is kept here. The shelves are full of books and magazines, folders, holders and envelopes. I decide to do some research on the open Porsche models while I wait.

Featured on these pages, the earliest open Porsches. On the left-hand page, Porsche Number One, on a street in Zurich, Switzerland. At this point, certain changes are being done; the bumpers have been removed and the wheel cut-outs have been given a flowing, more elegant line. The cockpit and the engine compartment are clearly visible in the picture to the right. On this page, top, the Beutler Cabriolet. This is one of two with a more sculptured rear and it is on display at the Swiss Museum of Transportation in Luzern. Beside it, one of two Gmünd Cabriolets, this one on display at the German Automuseum in Schloss Landesburg. The two pictures above show the America Roadster belonging to Robert Hicks of Oregon. (Photos courtesy Road & Track and Gene Babow.)

I see photographs from a place called Gmünd, in Austria, where the first Porsches were made. The buildings look like they were old already then; the plank walls appear weathered and cracked; the windows have panes missing and broken; the driveway is full of potholes and the grass is growing wild. Porsche had to move here in 1944 when allied bombing made Stuttgart too dangerous.

I see pictures of the first car. It is 1948. They show a strange-looking creation with a rear deck that's too long. But the characteristic sloping Porsche front is already there. It was a true roadster, with a flimsy top and without roll-up windows. There was only one copy made — in aluminum. Enter: Style 1.

Before this car was completed, work had begun on another, much improved and changed version. This was the coupe. All in all, less than sixty came out of the Gmünd production, all aluminum-bodied. Bill Jackson, naturally, has one of them — a coupe.

Six of these, in chassis form, were sent to Switzerland where convertible aluminum bodies were fitted by Beutler. The Porsche front is there, but on two of them, the rear had become more pronounced. The Beutler Cabriolet was Porsche's first true cabriolet, with a padded top and roll-up windows. Enter: Style 2. Bill is keeping one under surveilance.

In 1949, two convertibles were produced by Porsche themselves in Gmünd. These look like the later production Cabriolet, but have a different windshield and an aluminum body. Let's call it the Gmünd Cabriolet. Enter: Style 3.

The year is 1950. Porsche has moved back to Stuttgart, where production finally starts in a serious way. Now comes the 356 Cabriolet, its styling derived directly from the coupe, built by Reutter in steel, with padded top and roll-up windows. More than five thousand would be sold between 1951 and 1959, its body style basically unchanged. Enter: Style 4.

By now Porsche was trying for the American market. Max Hoffman, an independent dealer in New York, spearheaded this effort. He had strong feelings about price and styling. As a result, another open car was drawn up and built by Heuer, a sometimes supplier of cabriolet bodies to Porsche. The America Roadster, named after its intended market, retained the Porsche front but sported a new fender line, sweeping low at the cockpit, rising again above the rear wheel. I see pictures and it strikes me that the design of the cockpit area must have been strongly influenced by Jaguar's XK120. I look at the windshield

(continued on overleaf)

Final version of the faithful 356! And many Porsche enthusiasts would agree: The finest in sensible sports car motoring! The C-series was the result of fifteen years of refinement in the areas of handling, braking, dependability, performance, and finish – and in the case of the Cabriolet, it was topped off, so to speak, with an all-weather, fully padded top, made according to classic traditions. The 1965 model featured on these pages, chassis number 160909, belongs to Bill Jackson. An accomplished collector of all Porsches – not many models are missing in his stable – he still appreciates the basic, honest pleasures of driving his Cabriolet – last of a breed.

and the upholstery, the way it has been wrapped around the edges of the cockpit. The resemblance is even more evident in a picture showing the America Roadster with the top up. I feel sure Hoffman had told Porsche what a formidable competitor Jaguar was in the United States, especially coming in at a price of $3,300. I think Hoffman wanted a car with those features, and he got it, but he didn't get the price. The America Roadster came with a $4,600 price tag. Only sixteen were built between 1952 and 1953. This was due to Heuer's financial troubles, but also due to the fact that there was a new roadster under development — the Speedster. The America Roadster was aluminum-bodied and had a simple top and side curtains — a true roadster. Enter: Style 5. And, correct, Bill Jackson has one of these also!

The Speedster came in 1954. In this car Porsche and Hoffman had a price leader, at just below $3,000, as well as a style leader that was uniquely Porsche. It opened the United States market in grand style. The bodies were made by Reutter, in steel — except for a few aluminum Carreras — and it was a true roadster. Altogether close to five thousand Speedsters were made between 1954 and 1958. Enter: Style 6. Bill Jackson has three, right!

In 1958 Porsche gave in to dealers who felt that the Speedster was too primitive. It got a higher windshield and roll-up windows. Now called the D-Convertible — for Drauz, the builder — it was no longer a true roadster, although it still had an unpadded top. This steel-bodied version was made in 1,330 copies between 1958 and 1959. Enter: Style 7.

The basic 356 style was slightly reshaped in 1959. The top and window of the D-Cabriolet were applied to this new body. Around three thousand were made between 1959 and 1961, now bodied by the Belgian coachbuilder D'Ieteren. Although it was not a true roadster it was called the Roadster. Enter: Style 8.

The new body also came in the classic Cabriolet version. There were no exterior differences between the B- and C-series, except for the hubcaps. The steel bodies were made by Reutter in almost ten thousand examples between 1959 and 1965. Enter: Style 9.

As I write this, several months later, the phone rings. A reliable source confirms what another had told me: The Porsche people are definitely working on a new, true Cabriolet, based on the 911 and soon to be introduced in rendering form. Enter: Style 10.

The shooting at Red Rocks? Just barely made it, getting the usable shots of the Cabriolet on the last four frames of the last roll of film!

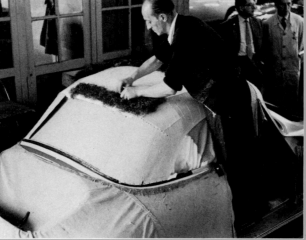

Porsche's series-produced open cars is the subject of this spread. The photograph above shows the 1961 assembly-line manufacture of Roadsters at the Belgian coachbuilder D'Ieteren in Brussels. To the left, a padded top is being expertly attended to by a craftsman at Reutters in Stuttgart. On the opposite page, first column, top, the 1950 356 Cabriolet, with its split windshield and flush bumper. Below it, compare the rounded windshield frame of the Speedster with the sharp-angled one of its successor, the D-Convertible, pictured at the bottom of the first column. Second column, top, the B-type Cabriolet. Exterior difference between this and the C-type was the hubcap. Next, a Speedster in action. At the bottom of the page, the 1960 Roadster with its simple top and roll-up windows. (Photos courtesy Road & Track.)

904 CARRERA GTS

The Last Road Racer

There's something about the styling of the 904 that makes it appear so light and delicate. It's the most strikingly beautiful of all Porsche road cars.

The 904 was a truly dual-purpose car. It was conceived that way not only to qualify it for racing — rules required one hundred to be built — but also to help pay for its development. It was the last time Porsche could offer a car that looked the same when raced in world class competition as it did on the road.

The 904 was styled with aerodynamics in mind, although, as a matter of interest it was developed without the aid of a wind tunnel. Later tests have shown it to have the very low drag coefficient of 0.33. What marks the 904 as a work of art is the harmony between the various elements of the body, the execution of the details and the overall expression of balance, power, speed and aggressiveness. It all reveals the highly developed artistic sense of the stylist — none other than Butzi Porsche, the son of Ferry Porsche and the grandson of Ferdinand Porsche.

While both Ferdinand and Ferry had chosen the field of engineering as their specialty, Butzi chose industrial design. He was appointed the head of the Styling Department when it was organized in the early sixties. Thanks to the infancy of this department and the urgency with which the 904 was needed, Butzi worked out the styling of the 904 virtually single-handedly. Without the often hampering effect of staff and committees, Butzi succeeded in creating a masterpiece — one that will always have a place among the great automotive designs.

But styling was only one aspect of the 904. What was hidden beneath its beautiful skin was more important on the racetrack. The 904 had originally been conceived for the new six-cylinder engine. But it wasn't ready in time for the 1964 season; the decade-old, well-proven four-cam engine was instead fitted behind the cockpit.

The combination of low weight — the fiberglass body weighed only 180 pounds — high-power output

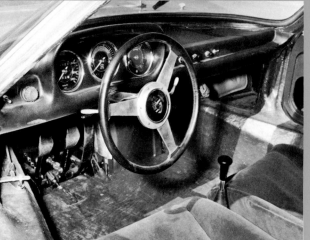

The fiberglass bodies for the 904 were built by the aircraft manufacturer Heinkel, and delivered painted and detailed. The picture above shows the engine and suspension being mated to the body at the Porsche factory. To the left, the snug and functional cockpit. The seats were not adjustable, instead both pedals and steering wheel were. The steering wheel shown in the photograph was replaced by an English-made Les Lester, wood-rimmed wheel in the production version. The engine, to the right, was the Fuhrmann four-cam unit in its biggest-bore form, just under two liters, and was very accessible once the tail portion of the body was removed. Above, right, the beautiful and efficient profile of Butzi Porsche's masterpiece. (Photos courtesy Road & Track.)

and low drag coefficient made the 904 a winner. During its two major seasons, it showed its superiority in all forms of endurance events. 904s unexpectedly took first and second overall in the 1964 Targa Florio. 904s placed first, second, fourth, fifth and sixth in class at Le Mans that same year. The next year, a 904 again took first in class. Also in 1965, a 904 surprised everyone by placing second in that year's grueling Monte Carlo Rally.

One of the first outings on United States soil was the twelve-hour Sebring. Five cars had been entered, but there was also a sixth present in the pits. It was chassis number 904019, belonging to Dutch privateer Count Carel de Beaufort. This 904 was his backup car. It took part in practice, but never raced.

Another newcomer on the track was Alfa's GTZ. One of the factory team drivers was Chuck Stoddard. That time at Sebring was his first encounter with the 904s, and he had an excellent opportunity to judge them in their true element, dueling with them for twelve hours. Three of the five 904s crossed the finish line, Briggs Cunningham taking fifth overall and first in the 2000cc class. Chuck was thirteenth overall and the winner of the 1600cc class.

Chuck grew up with cars. At the age of fourteen, living in Connecticut, his home was too far from school to qualify for bus service, so he bought an old Ford, parking it behind a barn since he didn't have a license. During his teenage years he bought, fixed and sold cars. In 1948, after having seen his first MG, he discovered that the world didn't consist of Fords alone. The MG awakened his interest in European sports cars. In college, he majored in automotive engineering, graduating from Boston's MIT. He was obviously preparing for an automotive career.

In 1952, he took up racing, over the years campaigning everything from a TD, a Jaguar, a Siata and an MGA to an Alfa Giulietta, an AC Ace and a Porsche 550 Spyder. In 1957, he opened a dealership in Willoughby, Ohio. He represented just about every obscure make you can name, as well as Porsche and Mercedes. He continued to be active in racing, adding national SCCA championships in G, D, and C production to his accomplishments. In 1964, he also captured the National United States Road Racing Championship for under two litres.

By 1965, his racing involvement had become so serious that the next step would have been to turn professional. It was that or the business. Luckily for Porsche enthusiasts, he chose the business. After

(continued on overleaf)

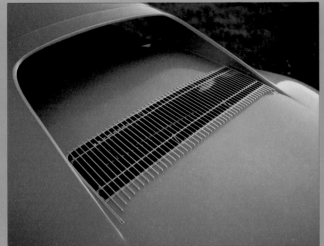

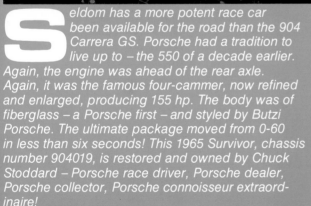

Seldom has a more potent race car been available for the road than the 904 Carrera GS. Porsche had a tradition to live up to – the 550 of a decade earlier. Again, the engine was ahead of the rear axle. Again, it was the famous four-cammer, now refined and enlarged, producing 155 hp. The body was of fiberglass – a Porsche first – and styled by Butzi Porsche. The ultimate package moved from 0-60 in less than six seconds! This 1965 Survivor, chassis number 904019, is restored and owned by Chuck Stoddard – Porsche race driver, Porsche dealer, Porsche collector, Porsche connoisseur extraordinaire!

having gradually phased out all other makes, he concentrated on Porsche. Today, his impressive facilities stand as a monument to dedication, organization and the quest for perfection. It must be one of the most complete Porsche organizations of its kind in the world. There's a new and used car dealership, complete with showroom, service and parts departments. There's also a restoration facility with engine and machine shop, body and paint shop and even an upholstery shop. There's a mail-order organization, with a 124-page catalog distributed worldwide, that specializes in parts and accessories for Porsches of all ages. Many of the older parts are remanufactured, carefully matching the original specifications. The stock of parts occupies a 2,000 square-foot area and consists of about 15,000 items. There's also a collection of vintage Porsches, the latest addition being an America Roadster, immaculately restored. A Gmünd Coupe is waiting in the wings. In addition to all his other duties, Chuck also served as president of the Porsche Club of America in 1979 and 1980.

It was in the early seventies that Chuck began to realize that all those historic Porsches would not be around forever, and if he wanted to own them, he better get them while they were still available. One of the models he had always wanted was the 904. Destiny arranged it so that the one he found, chassis number 904019, was one of the cars he had encountered at Sebring in 1964. Today, the 904 is immaculately restored, the work of Chuck's own hands.

We spent a most enjoyable afternoon together in the outskirts of Willoughby, the 904 resting quietly in a field of dandelions, waiting for the last afternoon sun to illuminate its silver body in just the right way. Chuck and I, in the meantime, discussed old Porsches, new Porsches, restoration and racing, and with those subjects out of the way, the drawbacks of socialism and the attractiveness of cats.

After the shooting, I was offered a ride in the 904 — I had to take my shoes off to fit — and discovered another of its aspects, besides the fact that it was very small. Its sound! When Chuck gave it full throttle, on the street in front of his dealership of all places, there was only one word that came to my mind — obscene! It was a sound that was in total contrast with the lightness, delicateness and beauty of that body. It was a sound that turned all heads. I felt like I was standing in the middle of Times Square during the rush hour, dressed only in my shorts.

I tried other words, but there was only one that could describe that sound — obscene!

904 prototypes were shown to the press at the Solitude circuit during the latter part of 1963, with prospective buyers also invited. In a short two-week period after this event, almost the entire planned production had been spoken for. The photograph at the top of the opposite page shows that the weather did not cooperate as willingly as the buyers. Above, the 904 looked good from any angle, but the three-quarter frontal aspect was especially flattering, focusing on the long nose and the beautifully shaped headlight covers. Left, bottom, notice the air intake for brake ventilation just behind the side window. On the production version, this was replaced by a scoop, visible on the 904 at speed in the picture to the right. The area hasn't yet been painted. (Photos courtesy Road & Track.)

912

Bit By the Porsche Bug

"Yes, Ray, you were definitely bitten by the Porsche Bug that time. Even though it took so long for it to break out, it was still the occasion when you got the affliction you're suffering from now!"

"You mean that time in Germany?"

"Yes, it has a tendency to affect you many years later. You're never safe. If you have the disposition, a bite like that will usually get you sooner or later!"

Here I am lecturing Ray Stewart, a doctor of medicine, on the effects of bites by the Porsche Bug! Presumptuous, perhaps, but we all know that doctors don't have the answers to everything. And I am, after all, well-qualified to give advice in this field, having myself suffered from the affliction for many years.

Ray has just told me about his first encounter with a Porsche. It took place in Bamberg, Bavaria. The year was 1956. He was fourteen then and lived in that German town with his mother and father, a United States Army officer. It was a family habit to go on an outing every Sunday after church. On this particular Sunday, as so many times before, they went to Schloss Bamberg, the old castle that had given the town its name. There, besides the beauty of the surrounding scenery and the intrigue of the medieval architecture, Ray's father could enjoy his favorite beer — the Bamberger Hofbrau — served cold in the Schloss Keller. At that age, Ray was, of course, only allowed a sip. Just a little for his education.

But it wasn't the Bug of German Beer that bit him that time, nor was it the Bug of Medieval Castles. No, it was the Porsche Bug. Yes, the dreaded Porsche Bug in the form of a low, smooth, streamlined 356, parked under the branches of some birch trees, resting innocently beside a cobblestone driveway, its round surfaces silvery in the summer sun.

Ray was impressed by the Porsche. But he didn't feel an immediate attraction. It was too different. He did sense that it was a car meant to be driven fast. Why else would they have made it so streamlined? It was as if they had not cared about fashion or what people liked. They had only made it look the way it

had to look in order to glide smoothly though the air. And he did sense that it was meant for the pleasure of driving. Why else would there be so little room in it? Ray also remembers that he was surprised when his father told him the engine was in the rear. Yes, the Porsche was too different for Ray's taste.

But, that was all it took. It was the first bite! Oh, yes, there was one more thing. Ray's father thought it would be a good idea to preserve the occasion for the future. Perhaps he sensed the importance of the moment. In the viewfinder of his camera he saw a unique sports car, sleepy-looking with its aftermarket eyelids, and he saw a young man, wearing a tie, his jacket a size too large so he could grow into it, his blond hair crew-cut, his hand resting on the door handle with a blend of pride and embarrassment — a young man just bitten by the Porsche Bug.

It was the summer before he went to Eugene, Oregon, as a freshman in college, that he had finally managed to save up enough money to buy the car he thought was his dream car — a brand new 1963 Corvette. But his best friend arrived at school in a new Porsche. And, to his own dismay, Ray found himself wanting to swap cars with him. As often as he managed to talk his friend into it, he took the Porsche for a drive, sometimes borrowing it for the entire weekend. Ray remembers how he felt that he could drive as fast with the Porsche as he could with the Corvette, perhaps faster, especially over the winding roads of McKenzie River Pass.

When the new-generation Porsche, the 911, arrived in 1965, Ray was disappointed to see that the price had risen to way beyond his means. But, when the 912 appeared soon afterward, his hopes of owning a Porsche returned. If it hadn't been for the fact that after having graduated from dentistry school, he immediately went back to school, this time to study medicine, he would have bought a 912 right away. Now, he had to wait until 1969. He still had to practice dentistry on weekends to pay for the Porsche.

Twelve years later Ray and I are looking at that same 912. He still owns it. We've just completed the shooting session. I had hoped for rain; it would have been decorative, and for a while the clouds looked very dark, but nothing came of it. The 912 is resting on the bottom of a dried-out riverbed, somewhere in the eastern outskirts of California's San Bernardino National Forest, just where the desert is attempting to take over from the mountains.

A replacement for the 356, first intended as an improved version of the aging classic, then becoming a totally redesigned vehicle, started its drawing board existence already in 1956. The engine was new, the transmission was new, the suspension was new, and so was the styling. It was the work of Butzi Porsche and his staff, and although the new style was fresh, slim and functional, the family resemblance was unmistakable. These photographs were taken during its premier showing at the Frankfurt Auto Show in September of 1963. It would take an entire year before customers were able to own one. Notice the small Porsche script and the twin exhaust pipes in the picture to the right. (Photo courtesy Road & Track.)

(continued on overleaf)

Porsche's second generation, the 911, was an all-new car with an all-new six-cylinder engine and a price tag to match. This made room for a less expensive version: the 912. It had the old economical four-cylinder engine, now further refined. The styling and handling were the same as the new generation. It was just what Ray Stewart, original owner of this 1969 912, chassis number 129023289, had been waiting for. Today, although having expanded his palate to include even the most expensive Porsches, he is still as pleased with his 912, still keeping it as it was when new – right down to the tires.

It's getting dark now and the horizontal rays of the sun are illuminating the familiar forms of the second-generation Porsche. I have always been impressed by the skill with which the stylists, under the direction of Butzi Porsche, managed to transfer the look of the old 356 to the totally redesigned 911. The old roundness was gone, a new sleekness was there instead. The front was flatter, the nose more drawn out, the roof sloping less, ending in a longer rear. The key to the shape of the entire design was evident in the shape of the side windows with its smooth, yet disciplined curve. The bumpers were well-integrated with the body, looking somewhat like the early 356. The blinkers and position lights were combined with the horn grill into a pleasing wraparound design that gave the car much of its fresh appearance; the same approach was also used for the rear blinkers and brake light combination. The new 911 was a far cry from the old 356. Yet, there was never any question of heritage.

Ray maneuvered the 912 out of the riverbed and I took over the wheel for a sunset test drive. The steering was quick. The front felt a little too light for my taste, but it stuck nicely in the curves, even when you pressed it. It was leaning a little low, and the front wheels were bouncing; Ray admitted that it might be time for new shocks. The shifting was a definite improvement over the 356, although with the five-gear layout I always ended-up going from first directly to third. The stick was shorter than on the 356 and had a more precise feel as well as a nicely shaped knob. With its less-powerful 356 engine on board, the 912 was definitely no racecar. But the sporty feel was there, and the looks — and economy too!

As we turn on the headlights, the sun now sinking behind the mountains, and swing the nose toward home, Ray turns to me.

"I think there's definitely something to that Porsche Bug theory of yours!" he says.

He tells me of how he has by now owned over twenty Porsches; everything from Speedsters to a 910 race car that raced at Le Mans. He tells me about a corporation he has just organized which offers to convert 928s to turbo-charged roadsters. And he tells me about another venture, just about to be started; the remanufacturing of the 904. It's going to be a faithful copy of the real thing, so good owners of 904s are going to be able to buy spare body panels. It's going to be available both as a kit and as a complete car.

"The bad thing about this affliction," I say, getting in a last word of encouragement. "The bad thing is that there's no cure. You just have to live with it!"

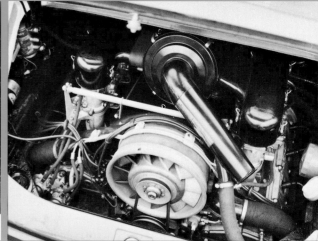

On these pages is a sampling from the first decade of 911 history. Left-hand page, top, a pre-production car. Notice the stubby look; the longer wheelbase did not come until 1968. Bottom, far left, the experimental engine in the Frankfurt showcar. Left, the production version. Left, center, the 1970 model – entering the period of the classic 911 look. They had the longer wheelbase, giving them that perfect visual balance; they had the forged alloy wheels, light and distinctively beautiful; and they still had the uncluttered bumper arrangement. To the right, bottom, the 1973 model, now with a front air-dam and new, less distinctive cast alloy wheels. Above, the early interior, here seen on a 1968 model. Above, right, the interior of the 1973 model, virtually unchanged. (Photos courtesy Road & Track.)

914-6

Road Testing For Real

1977 was a big year for Sam Cabiglio. He went to Europe three times, bringing more than fifty cars back to California. Eight of them were 930 Turbos.

One particular day in June of that year, we find Sam in Italy. We see him as he makes his way through heavy afternoon traffic in Milan, patiently maneuvering a big-winged, wide-flared 930 Turbo he had picked up at the factory a few days earlier. It is raining.

We see him as he turns into Via Frua, a street lined with mature, gray-trunked trees and century-old apartment buildings. Shops occupy the street level. Cafés sprawl on the sidewalks. They lay abandoned now as the heavy rain comes down with full force.

From habit, Sam's well-trained, all-seeing eyes scan every car he passes. Suddenly, he picks up the blue silhouette of a 914, parked in front of one of the shops. It is the five-spoked Fuchs alloy wheels that trigger his reaction. It must be a Six! Sam knows that those wheels came only on the Sixes! He also knows that very few Sixes were made. He slows down, turns around, and makes another pass. Sure enough. It is a Six! He finds a parking space, opens his umbrella, and ventures out for a dash across the street.

Sam looks the car over while the rain plays the drums on the tightly stretched fabric of the umbrella. The Six is very well preserved. And it is a 1971! Only about four hundred were made that year. Sam can tell that it is a 1971 from looking at the vinyl on the seats. This car has the smooth, leather-grained kind, as opposed to the waffle-perforated version used in 1970. He reaches for his red notebook, rips out a page and scribbles a message on it — all with difficulty, because of the rain and the umbrella — and leans over the car to fasten the note under a windshield wiper. Just then, the owner emerges from one of the shops. He approaches, his face wearing an expression of intrigue and suspicion. What is wrong?

"Per caso, la verebbe vendere?" Sam asks, holding

(continued on overleaf)

The 914 was obviously targeted to the young and beautiful, as evidenced by the publicity photograph above. Although the 914 did not have much room in its cockpit, it could boast of two luggage compartments. The removable roof-panel was another popular feature. When not in use, it was stored in the rear compartment and took very little space. The picture to the far right shows the sporty look of the cockpit – seats almost flush with the floor and steering wheel with a nice vertical angle. The 914 was also a potent racing machine. Left, one of the two 914-6s that came in second and fifth in the 1970 1000 kilometer race at Nürburgring. To the right, Dwight Mitchell behind the wheel of the Northern California Porsche+Audi Dealer's 914 in 1973. (Photos courtesy Road & Track.)

Handling was the primary strength of the 914; the location of the engine, ahead of the rear axle, gave it a nearly ideal weight distribution. When Porsche's six-cylinder, 110 hp 911T unit was installed, creating the 914-6 – it got power to match! Sam Cabiglio, purveyor of exotic Porsches, knew from his experience with a 914-6 in club racing the superiority of this combination. He found his 1971 914-6, chassis number 6420234, in Milan, Italy. Driving it to the limit across the Alps to Switzerland – the ultimate road test – further convinced him of its outstanding virtues.

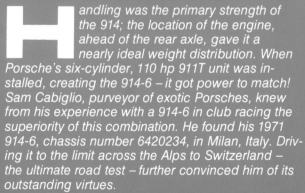

up the palm of his hand in a calming gesture. "Is the car by chance for sale?"

"Forcé!" comes the surprised reply. "Maybe!"

Sam was five years old when he and his parents moved to California in 1951. Cars were always the all-overshadowing interest during his childhood. But he had to wait until he turned seventeen before he could buy one. It was a Porsche Speedster, and it cost him two hundred dollars at the local junkyard. It came without an engine, but Sam soon took care of that problem, later selling the restored Speedster and using the handsome profit to buy a late model Coupe. He soon traded the Coupe for another Speedster, this one in perfect condition. He soon sold this Speedster too. Now the profit not only bought one, but two Coupes. A pattern was emerging!

In 1966, Sam earned a place in the spotlight when he put a Porsche engine in a Fiat 600. The combination worked so well that the promoters of the now defunct Lion's Dragstrip in Long Beach paid him to compete in a well-publicized run-off with a record-breaking Dodge. To everyone's surprise, Sam won! This resulted in a write-up in Hot Rod Magazine.

In the early part of the following year, Sam left for the first of his many buying trips to Europe. Among other cars, he picked up a brand-new 911S at the factory. On the desk of the man in charge of the delivery was a copy of the same issue of Hot Rod Magazine! It turned out to be the perfect introduction, and that first visit formed a basis for a continuing relationship with the people at the Porsche factory.

During the boom period that lasted from the late Sixties to the mid-Seventies, when certain models of great demand in California were still plentiful and cheap on the Continent, Sam perfected the pattern that he had developed as a teenager.

We return to Sam in Milan. Later in the afternoon, he reaches an agreement with the owner of the Six, and the deal is quickly consummated. Sam and his friend Mike leave for Stuttgart that same evening, where the cars bought on the trip will be assembled for later transport to California. It is agreed that Mike will drive the Turbo, while Sam will take the Six. Nothing is said about a duel. Nothing had to be said.

Their route to Stuttgart first takes them to Como, just north of Milan, where Sam was born. A short stop is necessary here to bid relatives farewell. From Como, they cut across to Lecco. The pace quickens as they race north along the shores of Lago di Como. Sam has a hard time keeping up with Mike here, but he knows, once they pass Chiavenna, his chance will

come. From there the road will shoot up into the mountains, winding, snaking, zig-zagging its way up the steep hillsides, cutting through the Splügen Pass and crossing into Switzerland.

The rain that had started in Milan follows them as they race on to the north. The higher they climb, the colder it gets. The rain finally turns into snow. But this proves to be the favorite playground of the Six.

Once on the mountainous section of the road, as Sam had expected, he is able to take over, passing the Turbo and holding onto the lead without difficulty. He is particularly impressed by the high-speed stability of the Six, noting it with special gratitude every time he comes shooting out from the dry tunnels onto the icy wetness of the uncovered roads. And in the curves, the Six really proves its racing heritage.

After Splügen, when the road again becomes wider and straighter, Sam has to give up the lead to Mike. They traverse Switzerland, passing through Chur and Buchs. Sam still in hot pursuit, they cross the border to Austria at Feldkirch, leave Austria at Lindau, race on along the eastern shore of the Bodensee, and continue on northbound to Stuttgart, where they arrive just before midnight, five hours after they left Milan.

I visit Sam Cabiglio at his place of operation in Long Beach. The building has a sign, but it is effectively hidden by the broad branches of a palm tree. It doesn't matter, because the people who count always know where to find him. Inside, you see a constantly varying assortment of Porsches — everything from racecars to road cars, from classics to the latest, un-imported models. And everything from parts and customizing to advice and enthusiasm.

We drive the blue Six to the Palos Verdes Peninsula, where I had found a beach full of pebbles. We have to do the shooting in the morning in order to avoid the high tide.

The sun comes up behind hazy morning clouds, just as I had ordered. By the time the shooting is done, the sun breaks through and it turns out to be another one of those perfect Southern California days. As we get back on the coast road, ready to do some testing, a marvelously curvy beach nymph needs a ride to Manhattan Beach. Sure, we can take that route. No problem. The European version of the 914 has a cushion between the two seats, making room for a second passenger. A thorough test requires everything to be checked out. And I can now honestly report that there is enough room between the seats to make it pleasant. There is one thing though, that seemed to pose a problem — the shifting.

The 916, if built in quantity, would have been the fastest production Porsche in 1972. The most expensive as well! Calculations showed that it would have had to be priced fifty percent higher than the most expensive 911. So, unfortunately, the eleven prototypes were the only ones built. The 911S engine developed 190 hp and gave the lighter car a top speed of 145 mph and a 0-60 time of less than seven seconds. To make room for the seven-inch wheels, the fenders had to be flared. Fiberglass panels took the place of the bumpers, giving the front and rear a very clean look. The frontal view shows a nice integration of driving lights and oil cooler air intake. The roof was made of steel and welded on for increased stiffness. (Photos by Bill Warner, courtesy Road & Track.)

911 CARRERA RS

The Champion Mechanic

Mention the name Vasek Polak to an experienced Porsche enthusiast and he will respond with a word of admiration, a smile at the recollection of an exciting race, or maybe even with an anecdote.

To the Southern California Porsche owner, Vasek Polak may be the man he bought his first Porsche from back in the fifties. It may be the dealership where he has purchased his subsequent Porsches. It may be the place where he has been going just to see what was new on the horizon.

To the serious Porsche restorer, Vasek Polak is a name he is well acquainted with. It doesn't matter in which part of the world he lives, if he is restoring a vintage Porsche racing machine, he sooner or later has had to talk to Vasek Polak about that brake drum or this crankshaft or those other hard-to-find parts.

To the observer of the Porsche racing scene, Vasek Polak is a name associated with the great drivers and the great races and the great victories. He will connect Vasek Polak with names like Bonnier, Behra, Miles, Ickx, Redman, Donohue, Schechter and many others. And he will recall the successes in SCCA, Can Am and Trans Am racing. So if you are a Porsche enthusiast, the name Vasek Polak will have been mentioned often. But it has not always been that way.

The unknown part of Vasek Polak's story begins in Prague, Czechoslovakia, where he was born in 1914. Racing and racing machinery was his main diet already in the late thirties; he operated his own machine shop, specializing in cylinder grinding; in his spare time he raced motorcycles. Photographs of the young Vasek show him on his four-valve Rudge, negotiating a curve with elegant style, leaning fearlessly, and after the race, wearing the victor's laurel around his neck with a proud smile, his leather jacket zipped open, his blond hair ruffled and unconstrictable.

In 1949, we find Vasek Polak in West Germany. He was first the maintenance manager for a United States Army repair depot, then ran a mixed machine shop in Munich. A brief visit to the United States in

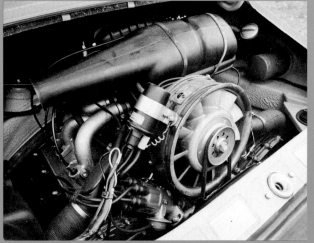

The first 911 Carrera to be marketed in the United States was introduced as the flagship of the 1974 model line-up. It had the ducktail, which improved stability during high speed as well as during cornering. But it was optional, as was the Carrera script on the body side panels. Also in 1974 came the new, higher and wider bumper design, necessitated by stricter impact laws. The accordian rubber joints became a visual eyemark of this change. The engine, as used in the Carrera, was still mechanically fuel injected, as opposed to the other 911 models, which came with the Jetronic system. The restyled interior featured new, lighter seats with integrated headrests, new door panels with larger, covered pockets, and a new, smaller, three-spoked steering wheel. (Photos courtesy Road & Track.)

1951 gave him an idea of where he wanted to settle. But it took another four years before a major obstacle had been overcome: that of getting his family out of Czechoslovakia. During those years he became involved with Porsches — a union of destiny. From then on he also knew how he would like to earn his living: He wanted his own Porsche dealership.

Vasek Polak and his family arrived in New York in 1956. A job awaited him with the Porsche distributor Max Hoffman. It did not take long before he invested in a car — his first on American soil. It was a Ford, and he paid twenty-five dollars for it. Of course, the Ford was for family transportation. For racing he had his eyes on a 550 Spyder. With his connections, he was soon able to buy one. In 1957, he took the Ford, the Spyder and the family and went west, like so many before him, settling in the Southern California community of Manhattan Beach. Soon afterward he was appointed the Porsche dealer there. His two immediate goals had been accomplished. The next phase could begin; the one that would make Vasek Polak a household word among Porsche people.

I open the heavy glass doors to Vasek Polak's Porsche showroom. It occupies an entire city block along the Pacific Coast Highway. To the right and straight ahead, I see rows of shiny new Porsches; 911s, 924s, 928s, as well as choice examples of used ones. To the left, lined up along the glass facade, their aerodynamic front ends facing that never-ending stream of vehicles passing on the highway, I see the cars that are not for sale at any price — the racing machines. This is only a small portion of a collection that has grown, not so much because of deliberate acquisition, but because Vasek could not give up his beloved race cars.

Vasek Polak was the name that came to my mind when I searched for a 2.7 Carrera RS to feature in this book. The model was not imported to the United States, so it is very hard to find one here. When I spoke to Mister Polak on the phone, he needed a few seconds to think, then he confirmed that he indeed had an RS sitting in one of his private garages. He had taken it in trade some years ago and had tested it himself at Willow Springs and found it both clean and strong. Ja, it is white like they all were. Ja, it has red wheels and red Carrera script on the sides. Ja, ja, it is okay to photograph it.

To interview Vasek Polak is no simple thing. First of all, he is nowhere and everywhere at the same time. And, when he does show up, unexpectedly from
(continued on overleaf)

Dramatic looks was just one of the reasons behind the appeal of the Carrera RS. True, the Carrera script and the color-matched wheels were visual effects, but the front air dam and the rear spoiler were functional, and together with the lightened body and the enlarged engine, responsible for the Carrera's exciting performance – sixty could be reached in less than six seconds. This Europe-only, touring-equipped 1973 2.7 Carrera RS, chassis number 9113600845 belongs to Vasek Polak, for more than two decades a name synonymous with outstanding accomplishments in the sales, service and racing of Porsches.

nowhere, you discover that there are at least three engines turning inside his head, all operating independently, all at the same time. One is working on the problem of the proper preparation of a particular race car. Another is wrestling with details of negotiations with a visitor from Stuttgart. The third, if you are lucky, is concentrating on you, unless the phone rings.

The interviewer gets in a few questions between phone calls in German, Slovak and inimitable English. The interviewer is trying to form a picture of a career that is so vast that it is hard to know where to begin. Who is Vasek Polak? What kind of man is he? Is he a businessman? An administrator? With an organization that employs more than one hundred people, and has been in operation for twenty-four years, he must be a very good businessman. But what else?

Vasek Polak makes an effort to cut out the phone calls. He leaves his chair, comes around his desk to sit in a chair beside the interviewer. He is stocky in body, strong-faced, shirt-sleeved, his blond hair from the old photograph, gray now, but still unconstrictable. I ask him what, during all these years, was best. At once, the other engines stop. He starts talking faster than I can take notes. Let the phone ring.

Best was Nassau Speed Week 1958. Graf Trips was driving special RSK for Johnny von Neumann. I was waiting in Nassau for car to come on ship from factory. When it came, I prepared at the Volkswagen dealership. After first practice, problem with engine. Could not be fixed. Airship another engine. Came night before race. Worked all night. How did you stay awake? Coffee? No, do not need drink or eat when you are excited. Where did you stay? Do not remember. Not important. Graf Trips had permission to drive two laps to check how everything worked. But no practice. In race, worked like a clock. Won overall. And at trophy presentation, everyone standing around, microphones, loudspeakers, Graf Trips stopped everything, took microphone, told everyone that Vasek here, without him it would never have worked'. Then he presented me his trophy. Still have it. Then a pause and a smile: That was best. Yes, all that was best! That is the answer.

The interview was over. Sorry. Phone calls in German, Slovak, and inimitable English. But the interviewer was pleased. He had received insight. He knows what kind of a man Vasek Polak is. He knows there is a great heart behind that facade of invincibility. A heart that beats for great drivers and great machines. Vasek Polak — champion mechanic of champion race cars.

The Carrera RS was the first phase in Porsche's production car racing program, started in 1972. The RS was based on the 911S, and one of the first concerns was to save weight. This was accomplished mainly by removing the rear seats, by making the body of thinner steel, and by using fiberglass bumpers. Another concern was to improve aerodymanics and handling, and this is where the ducktail and front air-dam played important roles. The engine, also from the 911S, was enlarged to produce 210 hp. Another element of the racing image was the Carrera lettering on the side panels. The first style can be seen on the prototype, pictured to the right, top. Before the premier showing at the 1972 Paris Auto Salon, the script was redesigned. Although only five hundred cars had to be built to qualify the Carrera for racing, slightly more than one thousand were completed and sold. Of these, approximately fifty were brought up to full racing specifications and called RSR. Pictured above, a racing-prepared 911S is shadowing a racing-prepared 911 Carrera RS. To the right, bottom, George Follmer in an RS at Daytona. To the left, Peter Gregg behind the wheel of one of his successful RSRs. (Photo courtesy Road & Track.)

911 CARRERA TARGA

Modern Day Outlaws

Try to create a picture in your mind of the representative Porsche owner. Early thirties. Successful businessman. Knows what is fashionable in art. In dress. In lifestyle. Knows how to enjoy it. You got it! That's Greg Jahn! But, while a man fitting this description usually owns one Porsche, Greg owns four!

Greg was always a sports car enthusiast. As a kid, he built models. As a teenager, he drove Triumphs. In college, he drove Corvettes. All this before he finally came to his senses and settled on Porsches. Greg lives in Cherry Hill, an affluent satellite-city of Philadelphia. His cars are maintained by Cherry Hill Classic Cars. Tom Hessert is the owner of this establishment, John Nelson the trusted associate.

Greg, Tom, John and I are seated around the best table at the best restaurant in the area. Greg knows how to pick 'em. Goes with the image. And it really is a very nice place. White table cloths. Matching napkins. Waiters with accents. And a menu so full of French it's tempting to just close your eyes and point. But Greg knows what it all means. Goes with the image. After the Coquilles St. Jacques is ordered, and after the Boeuf à la Maison, and after Baron Philippe's Mouton-Cadet 1976, after that, we get down to the business at hand. Porsches. I already know that Greg has an SC Cabriolet, a Carrera 2, a Carrera Targa and a Turbo. And I know that they're all sitting there in his garage. But I haven't seen them yet.

I'd think you'd have a hard time making up your mind which one to drive, I say. Well, in a way, Greg answers. I like 'em all, you know. But they all have their different purposes. Take the Cabriolet, for instance. That was my first Porsche. I drove it very much in the beginning. Then I spent a lot of money and time to restore it. It became a showcar. And then I couldn't drive it anymore. I got tired of that, so now I drive it again. I got the Carrera 2. Now I'm restoring that one to become a showcar. The Carbriolet is a car for that pure old-time, fast-but-comfortable pleasure-

Porsches last for a long time! The 356 was in production for a decade-and-a-half. The 911 has been around for nearly two decades, and is still going strong. Featured on these pages is the 911-look for the early Eighties. The 1980 SC, to the right, sporting both fender flares and safety bumpers, still has the basic look of the 1963 original. Above, the interior of the SC, with its three-spoked steering wheel. Left, the engine compartment. Right, top, the 1980 Weissach Coupe, a limited edition. Basically an SC equipped with front and rear spoilers, wide alloy wheels and sportier shock absorbers, the Weissach came in two versions, Platinum Metallic and Black Metallic. The interior was light beige with burgundy piping and burgundy carpets. (Photos courtesy Road & Track.)

drive, that open-air, Sunday-afternoon-type cruising. It doesn't demand anything from you. But it can do all you want it to do under those kind of driving circumstances. With the Turbo, it's totally different. True, it can be driven slow and without spirit, but I'd like to meet a sports car enthusiast who can resist all that power. So when you drive the Turbo, you find yourself occupied with the car. It demands so much from the driver. You can do so much with it. But you can also easily overdo it. Frankly, the Turbo scares me. I think that's a healthy attitude, though. You have to be a professional driver to really extend that Turbo to its limits. What about the Carrera? Now, the Carrera is something in-between the two, It's very fast. It's very comfortable. It doesn't scare you. In fact, it's a very forgiving car. And it looks great! It has it all. Let's go over it point for point, I say. Now we're all contributing to the discussion. We're all talking. Between bites.

First the tires. Right. They're seven inches wide in the front and eight inches in the back. On a regular Porsche they're six inches front and back. Right. The wider tires, of course, improve the traction and cornering. I use Dunlop Super Sports. They're squealy and noisy, but I like to hear it when I go through the curve. Good. And the wide wheels look nice too. Let's not forget that! Okay. Then the wheels. Right. They're the forged alloys by Fuchs. Just about half as heavy as the steel wheels on the 356. On the 1975 Carrera they're painted to match the color of that Carrera script on the side of the body. That looks very good. Okay. The flares next. Yes. They have to do with the wheels. You need those flares to make room for the wider tires. And they look good too. Then we have the air dam. Right. But we have to talk about the dam together with the spoiler. You can't have a car with only one of them, you know. Spoils the balance. Right. The dam keeps the air from slipping under the car. Keeps it from lifting. The spoiler keeps the air pushing down on the rear. Right. It all works together to hold the car down at high speed. And the side-wind stability becomes better too. The spoiler reduces top speed slightly, they say. But it looks good, right? Right. Let's not forget that. It's the trademark of the Carrera and the Turbo. And what's next? The Targa top. Right. That's very nice to have. That's the link to the Cabriolet. Not quite as nice as a real convertible. But safer. And you don't get as much wind. And it's unusual. There were only 172 Carrera Targas built in 1975. What's next? Are we running out? No. The black trim. Right. That became available in 1974.

(continued on overleaf)

Unique would be a keyword in a description of the Porsche on these pages: It's a Carrera, it's a Targa and it's gold on black. Only 36 were made! Owner Greg Jahn, a Porsche aficionado with a taste for the exotic, saw one flashing by during a visit to Hollywood, California. He knew instantly it was a car he had to have. It took phone calls to Porsche dealers all over North America to locate this 1975 model, chassis number 9115410024, in Florida. With its gold wheels and lettering, all-black trim, Targa top, spoiler, wide tires and flares, it has all the striking attributes of the breed.

Looks very good. Especially on a black car, like yours. I have seen Ralph Lauren's car and it's all black. Even has blacked-out windows. Looks really good. And the black with gold trim is very unusual. Only thirty-six of them built in 1975. Now we're running out of things, right? What about the all-leather seats with the waist supports? Right. They're very nice. And that fat, small steering wheel? Nice. Very nice.

Consuming the Boeuf à la Maison keeps us quiet for a while now. But we're soon at it again.

What about the police? Do you have any trouble? Yes, you almost have to be an outlaw to enjoy these cars to their fullest capacity. Right, modern-day outlaws. I remember one time when I was on my way home. On the turnpike. Was doing 120 in fifth. Cruising along. It was two o'clock in the morning. You know you're not causing another oil embargo just from going full speed for an hour or so. And you know you're not taking any chances in the middle of the night. No traffic. Straight road. No fog. No moisture. I was cruising along, doing 120. Suddenly, I passed a trooper. He must have been half asleep beside the road there. It must really have shook him awake to see me speeding by like that. But what could I do? It was too late to brake. So I just kept going. I knew he couldn't catch up with me. After about ten minutes I came to the tollbooths. They were all full of red lights and all kinds of officials were out there flagging me down. The trooper had called ahead on his radio. I just stayed in the car. About five minutes later, the trooper comes along, his lights and face about the same color. He said I was under arrest. And the car was impounded. They would get a tow-truck he said. Of course, I knew what a tow-truck would do to the Porsche. It would tear up the under-carriage. So I refused to get out of the car. It was all right to arrest me, I said. And it was all right to impound the car, I said. But I won't have my car damaged, I said. If you get a flat-bed, fine, but no regular tow-truck. We were arguing back and forth, the trooper getting madder than you know what. Then they were all trying to call for a flat-bed. Have you tried to get a flat-bed in the middle of the night? After about two hours, the trooper came back to the car. Just leave, he said, and make sure I never see you again. Just leave, he said. Yeah, it makes you some kind of an outlaw, doesn't it?

Well, gentlemen. Are we ready to inspect the monster? Yes, I am. Yeah, me too. Let's go. This was good food. Thank you. Yes, thank you very much. We feel like musketeers. Just the right mood for driving a Porsche Carrera.

The Targa was introduced in 1965. It was styled by Butzi Porsche. The two photographs above show the pre-production version. Notice that the roll-bar carries the Porsche crest rather than, as later, the Targa script. Deliveries of the new model began in the spring of 1967. At first, the roof-panel was collapsible and the rear window soft, allowing four different variations on the open-air theme. The fixed glass window and the ventilation slots on the roll-bar came with the 1968 models. The 1967 promotional picture to the left shows an attractive way of demonstrating the strength of the roll-bar. Above right, a 1973 Targa, seen from a three-quarter angle. Lower right, the side-view of a 1975 Targa. Far right, a 1979 Targa featuring the black roll-bar. (Photos courtesy Road & Track.)

930 TURBO

Too Hot To Handle!

The things I had *read* about the 930 Turbo intrigued me: The ultimate 911. The ultimate Porsche. An engineering masterpiece. The most practical of the supercars.

The things I had *heard* about the 930 Turbo intrigued me even more: Most owners don't know how to drive them. A very demanding car. An inexperienced driver who tries to drive it to the limit is a fool.

I was certainly most eager to form my own opinions about the 930 Turbo. But I knew I wasn't enough of a driver to give it a valid shake-down. Luckily, I knew the man who was: Pete Smith.

The Porsche dealership in Hollywood is located on Cahuenga, just a block off Hollywood Boulevard. A few years ago, when I first had a chance to visit the dealership's warehouse in the back, I saw Steve McQueen's Speedster in there. Last year, I saw Paul Newman's 928. Two weeks ago, I saw Robert Redford's 930 Turbo, brought all the way from Utah for scheduled maintenance. But this time, I was here for a pure and honorable reason — not to see star cars — to find out the truth about the 930 Turbo.

Pete Smith has automobiles in his blood. His grandfather was one of the first Chevrolet dealers in San Francisco. In 1939, his grandfather moved south to Glendale, where he took over a Dodge/Plymouth dealership. Pete's father inherited the business. In the early Sixties, he bought Johnny Von Neuman's Competition Motors, Porsche's early California stronghold, getting the Volkswagen dealership with it. Pete arrived on the scene in 1964. In 1969, when the Porsche/Audi union took place, more room was needed. The responsibilities were split between the two Smith brothers, Pete moving across the street to a new facility — housing Porsche/Audi — his brother concentrating on the original Volkswagen set-up.

But, being a Porsche dealer doesn't in itself make a man equipped to extract the full potential from a 930 Turbo. It takes more. Pete's career in racing began

The Turbo was first seen at the Paris Auto Show in the fall of 1974. The new "whale tail" spoiler had already been put to use on that year's three-liter Carrera RS, to the left captured during testing in Germany. Fifty of them were turned into full-fledged race cars: the RSR. In the beginning, the Turbo also had a three-liter engine, but in 1978, it was fitted with the three-point-three liter unit. The pictures on this page feature the 1976 version, its exciting profile seen above. With the introduction of the enlarged engine, the spoiler became higher and more squared-off. The picture to the right, of the Turbo's rear seats, is proof of the luxurious appointments. Above, a close-up of the Turbo's tachometer with its turbo boost gauge. (Photos courtesy Road & Track.)

rather innocently. He entered his Speedster in the first Historic Races at Monterey. He did so well there, capturing a first in class, that his appetite was whetted.

In 1977, he found himself the owner of a Porsche 908. It was the car Vic Elford had driven to a second overall in the 1969 Targa Florio. Pete restored it and decided to enter SCCA Group A sports racing. After having won seven out of nine races, he captured the championship in the Southern Pacific Region. So far in the 1981 racing season, his successes include a first in class in the twelve-hour Sebring. He was the co-driver of the 1976 Porsche Carrera RSR. He was also the co-driver of the same car in the twenty-four-hour Daytona, placing second in class. Le Mans is the next goal. Pete races for the enjoyment of it, he says. For the exhilaration of speed. For the satisfaction of the accomplishment. For the pleasure of having completed that perfect lap, when everything went smooth, fast and safe. To him, he says, the most demanding element of endurance racing is concentration.

Pete and I walk together through the service department, reaching the warehouse in the back. The Turbo is parked immediately inside the doors, in the front row, ready for action. The first thing I notice is the exquisite color. A metallic gray-blue. I ask Pete about it. Yes, he says, I specified that. It's actually a Mercedes color. The Porsche blue has too much blue in it, in my opinion, he says. I agree, I say, the silver with a touch of blue gets rid of that sweet, baby-blue effect. Makes it very classy and crisp.

Next, we open the doors and are overcome by that intoxicating aroma of leather. Yes, says Pete, I ordered it all in leather. Dash, door panels, armrests — everything. This leather is in the Porsche catalog. It's a tan-brown. The car is also equipped with electric sun roof, electric windows, air conditioning and stereo. Pete pushes in a tape — out comes Bach. Truth: The 930 Turbo is a luxury car. The fit, the finish, the amenities — not plush and fluffy — it's real, tasteful, meaningful luxury.

Pete gets in behind the wheel. He starts the engine. It fires up right away. It's quiet. Maybe disappointingly so. Even when we get out on the street and Pete gives it a little more throttle, it's quiet. There's a whistling sound when the turbo cuts in, but that too is hardly noticeable. That's characteristic, Pete says. Even as a race car on the track, the Turbo is quiet.

In traffic now, we're moving without any stalling, overheating, spitting, coughing or other typicals associated with high-performance machines. Anyone

(continued on overleaf)

Ultimate Porsche road machine! The 930 Turbo is the extension – to a seemingly impossible degree – of the original Porsche concept which combined sportiness, comfort and dependability. In the 930 Turbo, Porsche engineers mix their most advanced racing technology with their most innovative comfort features, creating a car so docile you can use it for everyday city driving, yet so powerful, a touch of your toe makes it leap from 0-60 in about six seconds! Pete Smith – race driver, Porsche dealer, enthusiast – is the owner of this immaculate 1979 Turbo, chassis number 9309801130.

can drive this car, Pete says, anywhere, anytime, as long as he doesn't try anything exotic. It's so docile, it's incredible! We're out on the freeway now, going north on 101. But watch now, Pete says. And I watch his foot as he puts the accelerator to the floor. Nothing much happens. It takes a second or so, and then suddenly, I'm thrown back in the seat, for the first time feeling the tingling sensation in my legs from the G-force. We slow down. We were passing cars left and right, like we had been shot out of a cannon. That's a danger, Pete says, the other drivers on the road don't expect a car they saw in their rearview mirror three seconds ago to be passing them, so they may change a lane or make another maneuver that causes trouble. Truth: The 930 Turbo is a tame street car, but it's also a wild race car. In the wrong hands, it can be a lethal weapon. The incredible acceleration that takes place when the turbo cuts in and the seeming effortlessness and quietness with which it does it, can easily get you in a lot of trouble.

We turn off the freeway now and onto Mulholland Drive, with all its sharp curves, winding picturesquely around the hillsides above Hollywood. Pete accelerates, approaches a curve, then brakes hard and turns on the power on the way out of the curve. He repeats it again and again. That's how you do it, he says. Slow in — fast out. If you don't brake enough before the curve, you'll have to steer your way around it.

·If you lose the rear, and you're experienced, you counter with the steering wheel and let the car sort itself out. If you're inexperienced, you'll let up on the throttle and then the rear will throw the other way, swinging from side to side — a situation that's almost impossible for the novice to control. The turbo engine doesn't have much braking power, so you have to rely on the brakes, not the engine, to slow you down before a curve. That's also why the 930 Turbo is equipped with the 917 racing brakes. Truth: The 930 Turbo is a demanding car. It demands that the driver has the capacity to handle it.

So, is the 930 Turbo the ultimate 911? Yes, most likely. It's hard to imagine that further development will take place. Is the 930 Turbo the ultimate Porsche? It depends. If you believe that a Porsche isn't a Porsche unless it has the engine in the rear — then, yes. But the rear location of the engine and the semi-trailing-arm rear suspension do have inherent problems not even the magic of the Porsche engineers can get rid of. Truth: With these basic problems corrected in the new generation, the stage is set for even greater things from Porsche.

Famous turbo-powered racing machines is the subject of these pages. To the right, top, the impressive rear view of the two-point-one liter unit used in the Turbo RSR. This version was not built on the 930, but rather influenced its development. Far right, two views of an RSR. They were raced in the 1974 Manufacturers Championship racing for prototypes and sponsored by Martini & Rossi. Above, the 934 prototype. This machine was built on the 930 Turbo, as can clearly be seen, and competed in Group 4 GT racing. The 934s of teams such as Kremer's, left, dominated the 1976 Championship scene in Europe. Right, bottom, the ultimate 930 development: the final version of the 935, competing in Group 5 GT racing. (Photos courtesy Road & Track.)

928

Eye of the Beholder

Just as I had expected, the location was perfect. The rough brutality of the dirty, blue-grey walls of coal, rising like mountains on three sides, obscuring sky and horizon, was a stark contrast to the smooth, clean silver shape of the 928. The Porsche represented the ultimate in technology, art and lifestyle on our planet, while the crater-like surroundings represented the outer-space-like void of life and beauty.

"It's perfect!" I tell Roger Gallet, owner of the 928, as I complete my first circle around the car, looking at it only through the viewfinder of my camera. For a long time, I have been intrigued by the prospect of photographing the 928. To see an object like a car through the lens of a camera is like seeing it again for the first time. And you're always curious to find out how it will look and what kind of effects you can create by choice of angles, lenses, light and location.

"Are you disappointed?" I ask Roger.

"No. Not at all. But I must admit that I was hesitant at first, when you suggested a mine. I had thought more along the lines of a golf course or a park. But I see it now. It's like the ugliness of the surroundings make the car look even more beautiful!"

Roger's 928 is the only one in Uniontown. The city is an old center of Pennsylvania's coal mining district, and people here have always lived a simple, close-to-earth life — a life far from luxuries like exotic cars. Roger's 928 is really an attention-getter.

The sun is having a hard time breaking through. At times, it looks like it's going to rain. But for now, the clouds, dark blue-gray like the coal, are keeping the rain to themselves. There's a barely noticeable shadow. I load the camera with a roll of 64 ASA Kodak EPR.

My initial reaction when I first saw the 928 was one of relief. Finally, the monopoly of "the Italian school of design" had been broken. Not that I didn't appreciate their creations, but it got a little monotonous when all you saw were sharp edges and wedge shapes. I was pleasantly surprised to see the roundness of the 928.

Moving at a pace slow enough to ensure the highest level of quality, the new 928 assembly line put out twenty-eight cars a day at the time these photographs were taken. It is a study in precision and a showcase of the latest assembly line innovations. While the 911 line moves from station to station at seven-minute intervals, the 928 line moves when the job is done. The facilities are surgically clean and the noise level is so low that visitors and workers can communicate in a normal tone of voice. To the left, the impressive power unit ready for its mating with the chassis. Above, a partial view of the assembly hall. To the right, top, a 928 body fresh out of the paint shop. To the right, bottom, the half-finished interior. Notice the electronic "brain" on the floor of the passenger side. (Photos Gene Babow.)

It was as much a step backward as it was a step forward. There was an obvious connection with the cars of the Fifties, and most significant, a connection with the ancestor of the 928 — the 356. The width, the swelling forms, the sloping front and rear profiles — all reminded me of the classic Porsche. It was a modern interpretation of the same concept.

"How do you like the headlights?" I ask Roger.

"I like them. By the way, they aren't unique, you know. The Lamborghini Miura has them too!"

"That's right. But I think it was an ingenious move to incorporate them on the 928. They strengthen the tie-in with the 356. Remember that flat, flounder-fish look of those early Porsches? Peering up at you with a slightly embarrassed expression? The 928 has that same look!"

"Yes. You're right! Never thought of that before. Those lights also give the front life. Most of the modern sports cars are too plain. I miss the expression of the headlights. You can't get that same feeling from grilles and air scoops alone."

Roger walks over to the 928, opens the door, turns on the lights and returns to our observation point. As they rise, they create a periscope-up feeling; or they remind you of an awakening monster.

"Here's another thing about that design. Thanks to the lights being exposed like that, they can open forward, which allows them to be round and aerodynamic, leaving only a minimal area out there in the speed-wind. Normally, you know, the lights are attached to rectangular flaps, which means they have to open backward, leaving those flaps in place during driving, looking ugly and catching wind.

The Porsche engineers handed the stylists a very wide engine. In order to keep it low, they had to make it wide. This created a visual problem. True, it was easier to make the front low, but to disguise the width took some doing. They solved it beautifully, letting the wheel wells swell out from sharp edges on each side of the car, those edges becoming the focusing points for the eye's judgment of the width. The stylists weren't as successful in hiding the bulk of the rear. Another, in my opinion, questionable solution is the shape of the wheel cutouts. Throughout the history of automotive design, we have seen that the most beautiful and aerodynamically effective approaches were the ones that closely followed the circle of the wheel. In the rear, where on the 928 the cutout is lower than in the front, it looks all right. But in the front, the shape of the cutouts leave large openings on either side of

(continued on overleaf)

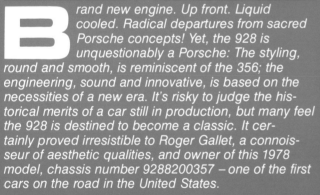

Brand new engine. Up front. Liquid cooled. Radical departures from sacred Porsche concepts! Yet, the 928 is unquestionably a Porsche: The styling, round and smooth, is reminiscent of the 356; the engineering, sound and innovative, is based on the necessities of a new era. It's risky to judge the historical merits of a car still in production, but many feel the 928 is destined to become a classic. It certainly proved irresistible to Roger Gallet, a connoisseur of aesthetic qualities, and owner of this 1978 model, chassis number 9288200357 – one of the first cars on the road in the United States.

the wheel, exposing parts of the chassis and suspension to the eye.

"It's perfect from the three-quarter front angle!"

"And it's perfect from straight on, too!"

"And from straight behind!"

"But not so good from the three-quarter rear angle. A little too bulky!"

"What about from the side?"

"I would have liked to move the greenhouse back visually, by having the wide panel between the windows slightly further back and slightly more upright. But we're playing a game. There are too many unknowns for us to suggest changes!"

"I know what you mean! It's like trying to pick apart the smile of Mona-Lisa. Every slight little change would upset the whole beautiful effect."

"But the rear light assembly is a real masterpiece. Totally unique, functional and beautiful!"

"But, of course, one of the most important innovations are the fully integrated bumpers. Can you imagine getting rid of those ugly bumpers that have destroyed designs for the past decade?"

"Yes, that's a relief. Remember the look of those early Gmünd cars, when they were raced without bumpers, and you could see all of those beautiful, round shapes? And remember the rear of the Abarth? The 928 has much of that same look! But I'm getting nostalgic now. Better get some shooting done!"

The sun still has a hard time breaking through the clouds. But it's lower now. And it creates a diffused light source so strong it erases some thin branches of dead trees that cling to the edge of the crater. This light is perfect. The right moment is now. I'm not saving film. Two hundred frames take less than half an hour. I'm shooting until the light is gone.

Somehow, news of our presence in the crater has spread. There's a small group of spectators; workers from the mine, boys on bicycles, and two old ladies. Roger has been keeping them happy by answering questions. Is it for *Life* magazine? No, Ma'am, this is a book about Porsches! About what? Porsches! Is it going to be on television? No, it's for a book! How much does this machine cost? Forty thousand!

"Why would anyone in their right mind pay forty thousand for that monster? Looks like a flying saucer!"

"Don't you like it, Ma'am?"

"Like it? I think it's ugly as sin!"

Beauty is in the eye of the beholder, as Toulouse-Lautrec put it when a viewer was offended by one of his paintings showing a lightly dressed female. Yes, beauty certainly is in the eyes of the beholder.

The 928, without question, represents a new level of accomplishment when it comes to a mass-produced sports car. It is outstanding in the area of technology as well as in the area of styling. The photographs featured here are ample evidence of the latter. The picture above, left, clearly shows the two sharp creases running down each side of the front fenders, camouflaging the massive width that was required to house the wide engine. Above, the 928's most flattering angle is this three-quarter frontal one. To the right, the driver's view. To the far right, a very successful Cabriolet conversion offered by Ray Stewart of Long Beach, California. The prototype conversion is the work of Gene Winfield of Canoga Park, California. (Photos courtesy Road & Track and Ray Stewart.)

924 TURBO

The Magic Show is On!

I had tried to get out by creating a rocking motion, quickly shifting from first to reverse and back to first. But I had only dug myself in deeper. Steam had been pouring out from under the car as the engine rubbed its hot belly in the mud. I had finally turned it off and stepped outside to survey the situation. The conclusion had been easily arrived at: I was stuck!

The 924 Turbo is brand new, swiped off the showroom floor at Carlsen's in Redwood City. I'm at the southern end of San Francisco Bay, where an intriguing-looking wasteland is reigned over by marshy fields and garbage dumps. I have taken all my shots. The sun is setting. I had chosen a different spot, closer to the water, but the Rangers chased me away from there. As if that wasn't enough, now I'm stuck. That's what I get for choosing exotic locations.

There was no traffic at all on the road. But there was a dump station about half-a-mile away. I had walked there to call for a tow truck. Now I'm back, sitting here behind the wheel of the 924 Turbo, waiting, the orange hazard lights blinking like the neon signs in a second-rate private-eye movie.

I lean back in the seat, trying to be positive, remembering the pleasant driving experience with the Turbo earlier in the afternoon. It sure stuck to the road. Those P7s are fantastic. They do make the ride hard and noisy, but the grip is great. And the turbo power feels good. Enough to have a reserve when needed. And enough to have a good time when wanted. Of course, it's not as dramatically aggressive as the 930 Turbo. Not by far. But it's not bad. The same whistling sound from the turbo is there. I'm not a test driver. But I know what I like. And I like to drive the 924 Turbo. But I don't like the finish of the interior. Not good enough for a $20,000 car.

My thoughts drift into the history of the 924. It's sure had a tough life. First of all, the Porsche engineers had to work with components available inside the Volkswagen/Audi group. It was the only way to keep *(continued on overleaf)*

The 924, and variations on that theme, is the subject of the photographs on the right-hand page. In the first row, top to bottom, three views of the basic 924. In the second row, top, the 924 Sebring. A total of 1300 units were produced of this limited edition. It was brought out to commemorate the choice of a 924 as the pacecar of the 1979 twelve-hour race at Sebring. They were all painted a bright red, with black, white and gold striping – the colors of the Porsche crest. Pictured below it, the 1981 924 Weissach. A total of four hundred were made of this limited edition. They were all painted two-tone Platinum Metallic. Below this, a 924 Turbo at speed, and to the left, its interior. Above, one of the first publicity shots of the new 944. (Photos courtesy Road & Track and Porsche Public Relations.)

Drag coefficient: among the best. Handling: among the best. Performance: among the worst. But with the introduction in 1979 of the Turbo, the 924 finally got the power to match its other attributes. It now produced 154 hp, reached a top speed of 130 and sported a 0-60 time just above nine seconds. Exterior give-aways were subtle: A small rear spoiler, two rows of louvers below the front bumper, air intakes (one on the hood and a row of four up front) and, optionally, the new forged alloy wheels with P7 Pirellis. This 1981 version, chassis number 93A0152125, belongs to Porsche dealer and avid Porsche enthusiast Charlie Burton.

the cost down. And then, when the 924 was ready on the drawing board, the Volkswagen people wanted it for themselves. It would then have been marketed as a Volkswagen or an Audi. But in the end, Porsche got it. Part of the agreement was that it should be manufactured at the Volkswagen plant in Neckarsulm. But Porsche would have full control. Well, on top of this zig-zagging birth process, when the 924 was finally introduced, it had a hard time coming across as a Porsche. Having a water-cooled, front-mounted Audi engine, and being assembled by Volkswagen, the skepticism of the Porsche purist was understandable.

But it couldn't be denied, the 924 had been designed by Porsche. And as such it had some basic things going for it. It had the engine up front and the transmission and gearbox in the rear, accomplishing ideal weight distribution. With the assistance of the new suspension, it all combined into one of the best handling machines in the business. The 924 also had that well-designed, moderately exciting, aerodynamically super-effective body going for it. Now, all it needed was some more of the Porsche magic — the same magic that had added another decade to the lifespan of the 911. The first number in Porsche's magic show was the 924 Turbo.

Another number was the D-production kit-racer. Introduced briefly into the 1979 SCCA season, it blossomed in the 1980 season, capturing fifteen regional wins and one divisional championship. This meant a much needed face-lift of the 924's anemic features.

But that wasn't all. The good old Carrera name was called upon again, effectively tying the 924 to the Porsche heritage. The prototype was first seen at the 1979 Frankfurt show. It looked great. I was especially attracted by the new interior. The idea was to build a car based on the 924 Turbo that would open the doors to Group 4 racing when the new FIA regulations became effective in 1982. With minor changes to the hood scoop and the rear fenders, and minus that good-looking interior, the four hundred cars needed for homologation were sold as the 924 Carrera GT; unfortunately, only available in Europe.

And as if the GT wasn't enough, soon came the GTS. A further lightened and refined version, still road going, the GTS produced 245 hp and was made in fifty copies. The racing version, the Carrera RSR, produced 375 hp the way it ran at Le Mans 1981, coming in sixth overall.

In that same race, another RSR came in seventh, powered by a new, four-cylinder engine. This unit, basically one-half of the 928 engine, produced 410 hp.

On these pages, a sampling of 924 derivatives for the benefit of increased adrenaline production. To the lower right, the prototype of the 924 SCCA D-production racer. To the upper right, the 924 Turbo Le Mans, a full-blown racing development of the 924 Carrera GTS. To the left, a 924 Carrera GT. This turbo-charged version was made in four hundred copies, unfortunately only available in Europe. Above, the extremely attractive Automotion Club Racer. This 924 Turbo derivative is the brainchild of Tom Green of Santa Clara, California. A fiberglas fender and spoiler kit makes it look good, and a suspension kit makes it handle as well as it looks. (Photos courtesy Road & Track, Gene Babow and Automotion.)

In its normal, un-turbocharged state, it's scheduled to power a new Porsche model — the 944. The 924 Turbo will be eliminated when the 944 arrives in the United States in the fall of 1982. But later, naturally, there will be a 944 Turbo, probably with an output of around 200 hp. And then? Well, Porsche's Magic Show is on! Who knows what's next?

The sun is gone now. I'm getting cold. And still no tow truck. Do some more thinking! Keep the spirit up! I remember the visit earlier in the day with Tom and Marjorie Green at Automotion. They offer yet another 924 alternative.

The Greens have been involved with Porsches since 1970, when they first prepared their Convertible D for club racing. The hobby soon grew into a business. In 1973, they started Automotion, specializing in Porsche parts and accessories, offering their wares through a mail-order catalog with worldwide distribution. There are now fourteen employees at the Santa Clara headquarters. That's where I went to see the 924 Automotion Club Racer.

It consists of kit components especially designed to make a 924 look and perform like a race car. It enables the enthusiast to prepare his 924 for auto crosses and time trials. The components are developed and designed by Automotion and manufactured to their specifications. The fender kit costs about $2,500, while the suspension kit runs about $1,500. This would bring a 924 up to the limit allowed by club rules. The prototype, where all the components are tested and developed, looks very good. Unfortunately, it had a run-in with a beside-the-road object the day before my visit, so it was temporarily out of commission. But Tom promised me a future test drive.

I'm extracted from my thoughts by the lights of an approaching car. As it comes closer, to my disappointment, I see it's not the tow truck. As it comes to a stop, four over-sized farmhands get out, moving slowly, looking like marauders, approaching the Turbo, probably hoping to find it abandoned. They look disappointed when I roll down the window, and even more disappointed when I ask them if they would help me get the car out. After a couple of half-hearted efforts, the Turbo is still stuck. I look in my pocket and fish out four twenty-dollar bills. Holding them out through the window like a carrot on a stick, I promise them one each when the car is free.

The experience returned my confidence in the buying power of the dollar. The Turbo was virtually lifted out of the mud hole. Naturally, I met the tow truck after only a few hundred yards.

"Porsches For The Road," sixth in the Survivors Series, was photographed, written and designed by Henry Rasmussen. The technical specifications in the content section were compiled and researched by Gene Babow. Assistant designer was Walt Woesner. Copy editor was Barbara Harold. Typesetting was supplied by Tintype Graphic Arts of San Luis Obispo. The color separations were produced by Graphic Arts Systems of Burbank. Zellerbach Paper Company supplied the 100-pound Flokote stock, manufactured by S. D. Warren. The special inks were formulated by Spectrum Ink Company of Los Angeles. Litho-Craft of Anaheim printed the book, under supervision of Brad Thurman. The binding was provided by National Bindery of Pomona.

In addition to the skilled craftsmen associated with the above mentioned firms, the author also wishes to thank the owners of the featured cars for their invaluable cooperation.

Special acknowledgements go to Gene Babow of Kentfield, California, Sam Cabiglio and Ray Stewart, both of Long Beach, California, Pete Smith of Hollywood, California and Chuck Stoddard of Willoughby, Ohio, for sharing so generously of their knowledge, earned over many years of involvement with Porsches. The author is also indebted to Tom Warth of Motorbooks International for his support, without which this book would not have been produced.

The author finally wishes to thank the following contributors: David Barr, Bruce Baker, Warren Eads, Gary Ellidge, Sepp Grinbold, Tom Hessert, Bruce Meyer, Otis Meyer, John Nelson, Rich Pasquali, Jim Perrin, Bob Raucher, Brad Riple, Joe Riva, Shirley Rusch and Carl Thompson.